Carried in Our Hearts

Carried in Our Hearts

THE GIFT OF ADOPTION

INSPIRING STORIES OF FAMILIES CREATED ACROSS CONTINENTS

Dr. Jane Aronson

JEREMY P. TARCHER/PENGUIN
a member of Penguin Group (USA) Inc.
New York

JEREMY P. TARCHER/PENGUIN
Published by the Penguin Group
Penguin Group (USA) Inc., 375 Hudson Street,
New York, New York 10014, USA

USA · Canada · UK · Ireland · Australia
New Zealand · India · South Africa · China

Penguin Books Ltd, Registered Offices: 80 Strand, London WC2R 0RL, England
For more information about the Penguin Group visit penguin.com

Most Tarcher/Penguin books are available at special quantity discounts for bulk purchase for sales
promotions, premiums, fund-raising, and educational needs. Special books or book excerpts also
can be created to fit specific needs. For details, write Penguin Group (USA) Inc. Special Markets,
375 Hudson Street, New York, NY 10014.

Library of Congress Cataloging-in-Publication Data

Aronson, Jane, date.
Carried in our hearts : the gift of adoption inspiring stories of
families created across continents / Dr. Jane Aronson.
p.   cm
ISBN 978-0-399-16105-6
1. Adoption.   2. Adoptive parents.   3. Families.   I. Title.
HV875.A73   2013   2013001138
362.734—dc23

Printed in the United States of America
1   3   5   7   9   10   8   6   4   2

Book design by Gretchen Achilles

ALWAYS LEARNING   PEARSON

To my sons, Ben and Des,

whom I love "infinity and beyond";

I thank them for their complete support

and inspiration for this book.

Contents

Foreword

My friend and mentor Jane Aronson has a dream. . . . That every child will find their forever family, that every child will realize their potential and every child will wear a broad wondrous smile on their face.

I am thrilled to have partnered with Jane on so many projects. We have powwowed on many a late evening on issues that need to be addressed. Her wisdom and experience have given me the confidence to continue advocating for kids. Jane has been a huge support for National Adoption Awareness Week in Australia, helping us to champion for a better system that will serve families and children. I am thrilled to be an Orphan Ranger for the Worldwide Orphans Foundation and to be on the board of WWO Australia, serving Australasia.

Jane works tirelessly pursuing her vision and following her passion. She approaches her work with such vigor, humor, and endless enthusiasm that you can only jump aboard her speeding train. There are so many of us now on board, and in these pages you will read about the abundant riches of experience from a diverse group of families who have all traveled a similar path.

Sharing our stories makes the journey so much sweeter.

—DEBORRA-LEE FURNESS,
founder of National Adoption
Awareness Week in Australia

Carried in Our Hearts

Introduction

I have been very lucky to have worked as a pediatrician advocating for children both in the United States and abroad for the past thirty years. I've watched as many of them have become members of permanent families who'd dreamed about their arrival, and their stories are as unique as they are universal in their depictions of love and familial struggles. Above all, I've always felt that these accounts of adoption should be shared with a wider audience—that these stories need to be told.

It has been a privilege to witness, over and over again, the miracle of a child who has traveled thousands of miles to join a permanent family grow, develop, and thrive in their new home. It has changed my life, and I am so grateful for all that the families I've worked with have taught me. I didn't know much when I started out, and I am not sure I was that credible. I was a good scientist, but then with their love and faith, I became a thoughtful pediatrician.

I have never stopped feeling the excitement of each visit with a newly formed family after their adoption; plotting the height, weight, and head circumference of the child on the growth chart. I print this chart out for parents so that they can take it home and look at it as proof not only of their child's health but of their good parenting. This can be of particular importance for adopted children, who often exhibit stunted growth on arrival and then go on to catch up over time in most cases. Being a part of a family's journey to adopt from the very beginning is especially rewarding. We might get together for a "primer" session so that the family can be guided in their decision of which country to pursue. Or on another visit, I might administer their travel vaccines in advance of their voyage to meet their child for the first time. These moments are very special for a family and being a part of them is gratifying. I am continually in awe of how vulnerable, devoted, and endlessly willing many of these adoptive parents are in their journeys to parenthood, and I believe that their stories reveal much about how to overcome the struggles that all parents face.

For many, many years as a pediatrician specializing in adoptive medicine, I was yearning and longing to be a parent just as these families were. The process of adoption can be painful and challenging, and I identified with my clients in their struggles because I was truly on the road with them. I also fell in love with the children; their vulnerability was palpable and their hurt was recognizable in their weak cries and their empty eyes. Often what I saw in person was not anything that I could have figured out from the pre-adoption report, and my feelings of sadness were deep yet inspiring; these little ones were so sweet and they drew me in and made me want more for them. I remember many times going to the restroom in my office and crying quietly, feeling the joy of witnessing these new families form. I longed to have my own child and be in their shoes. I was envious and happy for these new parents all at the same time until I ultimately adopted my own two sweet boys, Ben, now twelve, from Vietnam, and Des, now fourteen, from Ethiopia.

My practice has been a partnership with all my families in so many ways. We work together to get the medical and developmental issues resolved fast, and I want to be there for the families so that they will not feel isolated. Seeing parents step up and meet their responsibilities and be brave is so inspiring. I also value the moments when parents share their disappointments and confusion, especially about the early weeks and months of parenting. The joy of adoption is equal to that of birth, and so too post-adoption depression can mirror postpartum depression. I always encourage people to be honest about their feelings no matter how hard they might be to express. That is how families can get the help they need.

The essays you are about to read reveal how passionate parents can be about their children and how children resiliently defy the odds and pull themselves out of their sadness and bewilderment to become relaxed and content. They focus on various parts of the adoption process, including the decision to adopt, the endless paperwork, the waiting, the referral, the travel abroad to visit and/ or pick up the child, the early months of transition, the adaptation to home and family, the first experiences, the development, the relationships to siblings, and the many struggles some must confront on their journey together as a family. What struck me the most when I first received these testimonies was how perfectly they illustrated the struggles that all families go through, whether they include adopted children or not. Of course they revealed much about orphans and the tragedy of millions of children living without parental care around the world. But they also showed the resiliency of these special children and how important a family's love can be to any child.

International adoption has changed radically and has decreased dramatically in the last several years. Advocating for orphans in their communities all over the world through my role as the founder and CEO of Worldwide Orphans Foundation is now my calling. Adoption medicine inspired me to travel around the world to learn about orphans living in extremely poor countries who will most likely never be adopted by loving permanent families. I have gone on missions with other professionals to see firsthand how children are living in institutions. Sadly, I have witnessed tragic conditions for many often very young children, including threatened food security, severe malnutrition, homelessness, child labor, child trafficking, prostitution, little or no education, limited or no access to medical care, and dependence on orphanage/institutional care. These missions have given me a very raw look at this reality.

According to UNICEF reports, there are 153 million orphans in the world. Whether they are children who have lost one or both parents through death or they are "social orphans," meaning orphaned due to social, financial or health concerns, they are in fact children living in destitution with no parental guidance and no child protection, and it is tragic. There are two billion children in the world, of which one in ten may be at risk of being orphaned;

there are still more than twenty thousand children dying daily from completely preventable causes, half of what it was when I started medical school in 1982. The life of an orphan is usually depressing and there is harsh and abusive treatment by staff in institutions. Babies are bottle propped for their feeds and are rarely held. Solid food is sparse and kids lie long hours in their own excrement and urine while staring at the ceiling or their own hands, all the time feeling the empty and painful experience of hunger. There is little conversation from caregivers who are overworked and underpaid; they might have been kind and caring at one point in their careers but over time have become callous and then cruel.

I hope that this book will inspire more worldwide interest in and aid for these children left behind who so greatly need love and support. You will hear more in the final sections of this book about the work that I do with WWO as well as the work of others who have helped to improve the lives of orphans around the world—many of them inspired by their own adoption of a child from far away in another country to care deeply about the children left behind.

I.

The Decision

"My mommy didn't carry me in her tummy;
she carried me in her heart."

In this section of the book you will read about the many wonderful, unique, and sometimes surprising reasons why people adopt. Many assume that most people adopt because of infertility—and indeed this is one of the great gifts of adoption, that families longing for a child who are unable to conceive may build the family they have always dreamed of. But there are many young couples in their twenties who decide against having a child biologically simply because they want to save orphans and not overpopulate the world. Or other individuals—single or married, gay or straight—whose work or a vacation sent them to a foreign country where they fell in love with a culture and decided to adopt from that country. A newspaper story about the plight of orphans in Africa who lost their parents to AIDS can inspire parents to pick up the phone and begin the adoption process. A mother or father facing an empty nest with their children's departure to college might suddenly think, "Wait a minute, I don't think I'm quite done raising children." The death of an elderly parent could move a family to adopt and then name the child for that grandparent. Spiritual or religious moments have inspired adoption plans. There are many new families that form for such varied reasons that, frankly, nothing surprises me. What is universal in these stories is that a child who has never, or only briefly, known permanency discovers it in the loving embrace of a family—and this is what finally makes a child happy and healthy over the long term.

I always wanted to adopt a child. When I was very young, I saw those Save the Children advertisements on TV and I felt badly for kids who were very poor. I asked my parents to adopt the kids on TV. At one point—I can't remember the inspiration behind it—I asked them to adopt a Native American child, and they patiently explained that these children could not be adopted out of their tribe. That was disappointing, but more about that later.

In 1975, I saw a church announcement on an Upper East Side bulletin board advertising an adoption meeting. Being the youngest person at the meeting and the only one not married was uncomfortable. The church auditorium was filled with married couples who appeared to be mainly in their thirties and forties. The social workers running the event were probably my age, twenty-four. It was an informational meeting about adopting orphans from Vietnam. The American government was going to provide transportation for Vietnamese infants and toddlers who were being adopted by American citizens. I filled out an application and then we were given an opportunity to meet with a social worker that evening. They broke us up into groups and after they reviewed my application, they told me I was not eligible to adopt because I was single and too young.

That was called the "baby airlift" in April 1975. While I missed out on this opportunity, I put the flyer in a folder and continued to get mail from local adoption agencies in New York City throughout the years. I remember throwing away the file, which had become filled with brochures about adoption from Vietnam, Colombia, and Paraguay, years later. I was sad to give up my dream, but by then I was teaching and thinking about medical school and thought that there was no time for me to be a parent.

Fast-forward to me as a pediatrician specializing in adoption medicine in the 1990s. Off I went for a month's trip to China, with my then partner in life. I was the doctor on the trip for eight families who were adopting from China. It was a very cold and challenging trip, but at the same time it was a close-up look at the process of international adoption, and I was eager to learn so that I could be more helpful to my families. We traveled to Beijing and Guangzhou, and I took care of eight children who were adopted by eight American families. At one point there was a dramatic moment for one family that turned into a dramatic moment for me as well.

A baby scheduled to be adopted by one of my families was most likely blind. The adoptive mother suspected it the moment she first held the child in her arms, and she and her husband called me and the Chinese facilitator to their motel room to discuss the situation. According to adoption procedure, when a child was thought to be sick, the child had to be evaluated and assessed by a Chinese doctor. So we marched the baby to a children's hospital, where a vision test was performed and the child's blindness was confirmed.

With sadness, the family decided against adopting the child. They were fortunate in that the Chinese authorities agreed to place the blind child back in the orphanage and to provide the family with a new child. This was a nerve-racking moment because the papers had already been signed and the photos of the first baby were already on the visa, but the children looked enough alike, especially in their hairstyle, and nothing much had to be changed. The pain, suffering, and guilt the family felt were monumental, as you might imagine. The rest of the group was not informed, so that the family could process on their own without judgment.

My partner and I had to keep the blind baby in our room for a day and a night to manage the transition of the arrival of the new baby. There we were in a tiny motel room without heat and lights within a small, crowded, and polluted city in China, feeding and playing with a baby. It was a dream come true for me. My partner loved babies, but she was not interested in adopting; she had two grown children and was happy with our life alone.

I fell in love with this baby and still remember her sucking sounds as she eagerly devoured her warm formula thickened with oatmeal and topped off with a teaspoon of sugar—the same recipe I had instructed so many families to use to add much-needed extra calories to their children's diet and to help their babies sleep. I cried when I gave her back to the facilitator the next morning and spent many years grieving and pining for her. Fortunately, she was adopted by another family from the United States months later. The parents who had decided not to adopt her felt very grateful for their circumstances but also sad; it was one of those bittersweet moments in adoption. Their daughter graduated college recently. It is hard to believe this adoption occurred so long ago.

. . .

I finally came to terms with my decision to adopt and be a parent in 1999; I left an eighteen-year marriage to a woman and adopted a four-month-old infant boy from Vietnam in August 2000. More on this wonderful period in my life later. Many of the parents you'll hear from in the pages that follow had equally long roads to travel following their decision to adopt. Yet the joy that greeted us all when we were finally able to hold our children in our arms is, in most ways, indescribable.

MAGGIE GREENWALD

Maggie is a filmmaker. She lives in Maplewood, New Jersey, with her husband, David Mansfield, a composer, and their two daughters.

I decided to create my family through adoption when I was in fourth grade. It was the midsixties, and I ordered *The Family Nobody Wanted* by Helen Doss from Scholastic Books and read it instantly. Despite the unfortunate title—Doss had originally called her memoir *All God's Children*, though the publisher changed it before it was released in 1954—the book's an inspiring memoir of Helen and Carl Doss's adoption of eleven mixed-race children in the 1930s and 1940s. Though I lost my copy during various moves, and the book is now long out of print, I never forgot it. That was the kind of family I wanted.

At ten, the age my youngest daughter is now, I knew I wanted ten children. The number decreased as my years increased. By the time I was a young adult, I was a career-obsessed artist. I thought I'd never marry and assumed I would be a single mother. By twenty-five, one child seemed the right number. But who that child might be and where he or she might come from were both things I hadn't thought about. The first internationally adopted child I met was a blond-haired, blue-eyed boy from Romania adopted by a film producer I knew. Though he was adorable, I knew this wasn't my path.

At thirty-six, I'd just finished writing and directing my third feature film, and the time for motherhood seemed to be approaching. I had a friend who did work with orphanages in Cambodia, and I thought perhaps that would be my path. My heart began to pull me toward Asia, like a compass seeking true north.

And then the most unexpected thing of all happened—I met and fell in love with a man who would soon become my husband. For the first time, it occurred to me to have a biological child. I was getting older, though, and so my plan became to have a child and *then* adopt a child. But first, to make another movie.

When my husband and I started trying to conceive, I was forty. A year later, I still wasn't pregnant, but I'd become very aware of the sight of little Asian girls with Caucasian parents around New York City. When I learned these were Chinese daughters, abandoned by parents who wanted sons, I knew where my path to parenthood lay. As a lifelong feminist, I'd always railed against the inequality and injustices toward women—and so now, it only made sense that such passions would direct me to where I found my babies. (To this day, nothing causes me greater outrage than the preference for boys and the wholesale genocide of girls in some cultures.)

By day we began a brief foray into the demoralizing world of fertility treatments, and by night we researched China adoption. The fertility process was bizarre at best, humiliating at worst. Meanwhile, the packets from adoption agencies that began to arrive in the mail thrilled me. One day, while walking through the Union Square Greenmarket with my husband, I told him that even if I did conceive, I wanted to continue our adoption process. My feet were already on the road to China. I was committed. My husband nodded sagely—he knew when to say nothing.

We began the adoption process at the same time I was giving myself injections in preparation for an IVF procedure. So I reacted with a peculiar mix of indignation and relief when my fertility specialist told me I had produced only one follicle and that my few remaining eggs were "the dregs." Was I disappointed? Truthfully, not at the time—though now I do miss never having experienced pregnancy. I ran headlong and heart-long into the adoption process.

Where was my husband in all this? Walking beside me, though it wasn't a path he ever imagined. He's the father of an eleven-year-old from a previous marriage, and his daughter's face is a unique but recognizable blend of her mother's family's features and his own. He couldn't imagine what this new kind of family might look like. The adoptees we both knew when we were growing up seemed to fit nicely into their white families, often passing as their own biological children. Why was I so set on adopting a girl from China? Why not a white baby from the good ol' U.S.A.? Because in the deepest part of my soul, I knew that the child, or children, meant for me was the unwanted girl on the other side of the world.

Conveniently, serendipitously, I ran into an old acquaintance who had a two-year-old daughter, Maya, adopted from China. My friend invited us over for a visit. Skeptically, indulgently, David agreed to go. It was a cold rainy night, and as we walked to their loft, I was so excited that I kept tripping on cracks in the sidewalk. After introductions at the door, and with no prodding at all, bright, beautiful, and haughty Maya took David's hand and led him into her house. I stumbled happily into the loft behind them. I thought to myself, "Deal closed!"

We filed our paperwork. Over the months of waiting, I went to every meeting of the newly formed Families with Children from China (FCC). There were so many babies and toddlers there. I would weep, looking at that exquisite sea of faces. I remember hearing Dr. Jane Aronson talk for the first time to a room full of eager parents concerned about the possible health issues that face internationally adopted children. "When it comes to international adoption, all bets are off," she said with characteristic frankness. Undaunted and defiant, I never worried. CCAA, China Center of Adoption Affairs, changed the rules and regulations from time to time. Suddenly, because David had a child, the CCAA ruled that I already had one too. Due to their own one-child policy, China decided to apply their laws to foreign adoptive families, and we were a couple who already had their allocated child. Would they take my baby away before I had her? Our social worker, Patti Gross, reassured me, "Adoption is about faith." I sweated.

When our referral came nine months later, I couldn't believe it. My father, the towering patriarch of my family, was born on December 7. I have a niece born on the same day. More than half the members of my family have December birthdays. And here was the picture of my daughter, Mao Xiao Biao, Maisie, who was born on December 3 and had been found on December 7. She was five months old. It was meant to be! I went shopping for baby clothes.

We flew to Guangzhou, China, and then to Zhanjiang. From there we took a van with six other couples along a bumpy one-lane road, passing rice paddies and wooden carts pulled by water buffalo, to provincial Maoming. I wept during the entire three-hour drive. Another parent-to-be nicknamed me The Wreck. Never in my life have I been so filled with expectation. Never before have I had a feeling of fulfilling my destiny. As we arrived at the small, bleak notary's office, a group of women holding babies, our babies, rushed inside as we approached.

Martin, our cheerful facilitator, led us into the building's entryway but no farther. Then began a beautiful ritual in which each couple was called forward to be presented with their child, while the other families stood near sharing and savoring the moment. I started out as the group videographer, extracting a promise from one father to videotape the moment when my daughter and I were united. Of course, his baby was presented first. He was so nervous that when our baby was presented, he turned the camera off instead of on. Through my tears, I only saw my daughter. I don't know who brought her to me. She was placed in my arms and I could barely speak. In all the photos that were taken from that day, my eyes are red from crying. I wept, I smiled, and I kissed her small hand. She was awestruck, and so beautiful, her large dark eyes implacable as they took it all in. After a few moments, I handed her to David so I could see her, all of her. Here you are, my child. I have come to the ends of the earth for you. This was the journey I'd been waiting to take since I was ten years old.

I took many of the pictures that day while David held Maisie. I wanted to record everything so that when she was older, she'd have keepsakes from that day. About twenty minutes after we got our babies, we were waiting in the notary's office to finalize the adoptions. I was holding Maisie when David took a picture of the two of us that remains my favorite. We are looking at each other, and I'm smiling through my tears, drinking her in. Her large dark eyes gaze deeply into mine. We're soul meeting soul. Later that night, back at our hotel, Maisie slept lying on David's chest. He said, "It'll be good to come back in a few years and get Maisie a sister." Deal closed!

Three years later, we returned to China and brought home our daughter Lulu. Receiving her was another incredible experience, though very different. Lulu's foster mother, Pei Bao Hong, brought her to us. She also brought a bag of gifts: tiny mandarin oranges that Lulu loved, a large slice of angel food cake, eight eggs from her farm, and a bag of sugar for Lulu's formula. She had been paid eight dollars a month to care for this baby, whom she had grown to love.

Lulu was sobbing with fear when we met. Pei Bao Hong and I passed her back and forth for half an hour as we talked through the interpreters. As Lulu grew calm, I realized her gaze was fixed on her sister, Maisie.

A few years ago, I found a copy of *The Family Nobody Wanted* on eBay. I bought the original edition—the same Scholastic version that I'd read in fourth grade. On the cover are sketches of half a dozen children of different ages and races. They're surrounding the central image, a woman with short black hair holding a small baby wrapped in a blanket. It looks just like the photo of Maisie and me in the notary's office in Maoming, China, taken thirty-one years after I opened Helen Doss's book.

SHAZIA KHAWAJA

Shazia Khawaja is a lawyer and lives in Singapore with her husband and two daughters, Zayna and Anya.

The decision to adopt was not a difficult one for me. I always knew that the most important bond between a mother and a child is developed when you raise the child and not by giving birth. However, the logistics of adopting from Pakistan seemed daunting. Like most other Muslim countries, Pakistan does not recognize adoption and only grants guardianship to parents of an adopted child. Apart from the legal issues, most children are adopted directly from hospitals and do not get placed into orphanages. So the waiting lists at the orphanages are extremely long. Many people advised me not to adopt from Pakistan and instead go for an open adoption in the United States. Both my husband and I are Pakistani, and we were determined to adopt from Pakistan; we decided that we would do so no matter how difficult the process was going to be. It was a blessed decision in every way.

Six months after we had put our names down on the waiting list, we received a call from the orphanage to tell us that there was a beautiful baby girl who was perfect for us in every way. They wanted us to meet her a month later. I was warned that it could take up to six months before I could bring the baby back to New York. Undeterred, we made our plans and I went shopping for all the things that the baby could possibly need for the following four to six months. I had already decided that I would stay in Pakistan for whatever length of time was required.

We arrived in Karachi on September 23, 2003, and went to see the baby the very next day. I was filled with nervous excitement. We walked into the conference room in the orphanage. There were ten or twelve women sitting around a conference room table, but there was no baby in sight. A few minutes later, one of the caregivers brought a little baby girl into the room. She was wearing a white cotton smocked dress and was just beautiful. I told myself that I could not get attached, not just then. We took the little baby to the pediatrician that afternoon. As the doctor examined her, she grabbed my fingers and I knew at that very moment that no matter what transpired, we were meant to be mother and daughter. The decision was made.

Most adoption stories are filled with angst and anguish. That was not the case here, as all the stars were aligned for us. My childhood friend's mother was a preeminent family lawyer in Karachi. She navigated us through the complicated legal process, and we were able to get a guardianship order in a matter of weeks. Next, we had to go through the U.S. immigration process. My best friend from law school was in the foreign service, and one of her friends was based in the embassy in Islamabad. He was incredibly helpful and held our hands through that process. We were ready to leave.

There was still one piece that remained. I had to see the place where my daughter was born. I went to the hospital filled with trepidation. The head of the pediatric unit first met with me in his office. I asked if I could see the nursery where my daughter spent her first three days. He thought that it was an odd request but complied. I expected to be taken into a bare, institutional-type nursery—it was a government-owned hospital after all. Instead I walked into an impeccably clean yellow room with the most beautiful mural on the walls. I was told that a local artist had painted the mural. I felt that I had walked into Alice's Wonderland. It was simply magical.

Zayna and Anya, August 2012

SUZANA PERIC

*Suzana works in the film industry as a music editor. She has
resided in New York for the last thirty years, though she is
originally from Croatia. Lana, her daughter adopted from
Russia, is growing up in Manhattan in a bilingual household,
fluent in Croatian and English.*

My story began at 151 East 62nd Street on a winter afternoon back
in 2003.

I was in the doorway of Dr. Aronson's office, clumsily trying to
explain my reason for coming. Just as I was about to sit down, I
was caught in midair by her resolute tone of voice, correcting my
sentence:

"Not *if* you adopt, Suzana, but *when* you adopt."

I walked out of the office trying to grasp what just happened. I
knew at that point there was no turning back. This was my new
life and I was about to face it.

I knew I wanted to adopt internationally. Being an immigrant
myself, I made a list of countries I loved or would love to spend
time in, cultures I gravitated toward and felt kinship with. (Croatia,
my birthplace, didn't and still doesn't accept international adoptions.)

Also, approaching fifty, I wanted to adopt an "older" child.
That, I learned, is the term for a three-year-old.

I began the usual procedure of finding an adoption agency.
I started to learn about the process, eventually accepting that I
wouldn't be the one to find my child—rather, my child would find

me. After social worker searches, bank statements, medical check-ups, proof of everything I could think of proving, and an insur-mountable amount of paperwork, I was assigned to Brazil. Then the wait and the hope and the uncertainty.

Reading books on the subject scared me. They were full of warnings, advice, and scary stories. I wasn't ready for it all to be real, but time was running out so fast. Then I found out about an international adoption class led by Dr. Aronson. It met once a month for six months, which was the perfect pace for me; I could attend classes while also living a life in which I was comfortable. Change is a strange thing. We strive for it and yet it scares us more than anything. Daily routines were very important for me. My work was important; my friends were important; my dinner parties, con-certs, and theater were all so very important. And now these classes became part of my routine as well. The time between the monthly meetings was the most inspiring. I found myself being less scared, more practical, and more excited, and I realized why: I was learning. Knowing brings a sense of security.

Logistically, though, nine months of waiting had passed with-out any progress. In Brazil, there were complicated laws that were changing all the time, so the decision to move on to another coun-try seemed the right choice. Colombia was next. Again, laws changed just after I applied: no single parents, and no adoption allowed to people older than forty-five.

Next stop: Lithuania. By this time, a year had gone by, but I was still very positive about the process—I deeply believed that this was my destiny. Geographically, I was moving closer to the land of my origins, and I thought the end was in sight. Reports from the local lawyer were very positive. Until one day when he stopped returning my calls. Something was very wrong. The laws had changed, I found out. They'd stopped accepting applications from single parents. Another year had gone by.

Crushed? Yes. Disillusioned? Yes. But the idea that I'd give up because of a bureaucratic decision—in other words, giving up because someone else said so—was unacceptable.

I called Dr. Aronson and I found a new adoption agency that specialized in Russian adoption. There was no stopping me now. I had barely exchanged an e-mail or two with Jill, the agency staffer who was taking on my case, when my work took me to Paris.

I remember very well that first week in Paris. It was April of 2005 and I was working on a screen adaptation of *Oliver Twist*. Jill wrote to say that she might have a surprise very soon. And then, the very next day, there it was: I glanced at my e-mail and there was a note from Jill with an attachment included. It was early morning and no one was in the studio yet. I waited a moment, trying to catch my breath, before finally finding the courage to move the cursor to her e-mail and click it. . . .

A photograph popped up and I gasped. It was her—that child I had always been waiting for. There was something familiar about that wonderful face—it was beautiful, and very curious. I felt like I knew her, somehow, from somewhere. It was the most gorgeous April in Paris.

On April 15, 2006, Lana and I landed hand in hand in New York to begin our new life together, forever.

SHARI HERSHON

Shari is a fashion designer and editor. She lives in New York with her husband, photographer Spencer Jones, and their daughter, Bailey.

My husband felt the tug years before I did—that burning desire to have a child and become a parent. But then, when I was finally ready as well, we found ourselves unable to conceive.

It's a frustrating moment when you are in a loving and highly successful couple with the means to give a child a wonderful and rich life, but you are coming up empty.

After doctor appointments and exploring the options in modern fertility treatments, the realization hit me: I didn't care about procreating. I just wanted to be a parent.

Almost two years later, we adopted a beautiful baby girl from China.

I can't imagine loving a child more. Bailey has been the light of our lives from the moment we laid eyes on her. During the long and heart-wrenching wait to meet our daughter, I fell deeply in love with the idea of a wonderful little girl who would bring great joy to our lives. The magical moment when they brought her to us from the orphanage is one I'll never forget: it was the moment when I became a parent.

We have always spoken openly with Bailey about her adoption. We explain how the person who carried her couldn't keep her, so she went to the orphanage and they cared for her until we could come for her.

Somehow, children seem to grasp both the simplicity and complexity of situations with a wisdom and clarity that's well beyond their years.

One day, when she was about five years old, I heard her talking to a young friend about where she came from. Bailey very matter-of-factly summed up her situation by saying: "My mommy didn't carry me in her tummy; she carried me in her heart."

MOLLY WENGER MCCARTHY

Molly Wenger is the proud mom of Sam, Lulu Birtukan, and Loch. She lives in New Jersey with her children and her beloved better half, Mitch. They dream of adopting again.

My husband was a teenager when we met in college. As an older, more astute woman (of two whole years), I was disarmed immediately on our first date when I discovered that his life experience and future plans completely outshone mine (and I thought I was ahead of the game for already picking a major, damn it). After only knowing him for a few hours, he announced that he was adopted and that one day when he started his own family, he would adopt a child too. Truth be told, I loved him on the spot. Sold, sold, and sold. As our relationship grew, adoption became part of our foundation and our blueprint. It was in our hearts and minds when we nervously stood in front of each other and exchanged wedding vows in front of everyone we loved dearly. The seed was planted. We were on our way.

A quick aside: we dated for nine years before getting married. And for a woman who designed wedding flowers for a living, these were like dog years. The reason for the delay: he's Jewish and I'm Catholic. After obvious familial discontent and waves of disapproval from our loved ones, we postponed our two worlds colliding until after he got down on one knee. Our parents then awkwardly met at an Italian restaurant in Manhattan over pasta and palpable tension. This was assuredly our biggest hurdle in life to date.

So to our half-Jewish, half-Catholic, Irish, Native American,

Russian, and Polish by family heritage, Ethiopian-born daughter, Lulu Birtukan Poppy Wenger: you are braver, bolder, and worldlier at age two than your mommy and daddy will ever be in this lifetime or the next!

We gave birth to our son Samuel three years after we were married. As first-time parents, we were brimming with so much love, enthusiasm, sleep deprivation, delirium, and naïveté that we decided to start trying for a second baby immediately. Fast-forward three years later, and we had endured one lost beloved parent, one lost pregnancy, and many rounds of sex where the foreplay involved thermometers, watches, and mutual annoyance. We had officially arrived at a place of sadness, and we were most definitely stalled out. We always said we would adopt our last baby, but as the last of seven children and a member of the Irish Catholic fertile elite, I thought that would be around child number four, five, or even six! There was about to be a slightly sobering change of plans—it was now time to diverge and fast-forward a bit to adoption.

After research, lists, and even more lists, I found myself continually seeking solace in a beautiful webinar about Ethiopian adoption created by our adoption agency. It was my happy place and the personal draw was undeniable. This beautiful country and its gorgeous people drew me in every single time. A choice was emerging and with every click of my mouse I was falling in love with the plan. Most important, a never-seen-before confidence was taking hold in my former people-pleasing self. Our hearts and guts were now in control. We were starting to believe in that which we could not see. We didn't care about the noise around us. We knew we were ready.

We plodded through the paperwork with blood, sweat, tears, and care in a manner that I'm sure has been compared to labor in the adoption world, because, really, it's just that. I spent my birthday being fingerprinted in Newark, New Jersey, and it was the best way I have ever marked the passage of a year. We creepily talked a notary into accompanying us to our doctor's office because we thought the notes from our physicals needed to be notarized on the spot (they didn't). We laughed, cried, daydreamed, fought, signed, and notarized some more until we were finally waiting. That's the easy part, right? Wrong. Idle hands are the devil's workshop, they say, but so are waiting minds. We embarked on the high seas of paranoia and tension.

Then, in July of 2009, I almost ran my car off the road when I heard the words "match" and "daughter" from our agency. She was real. It was happening. Sweet Lu.

Three months later, in September, we left our home and our son and flew to Addis Ababa, Ethiopia, to meet our seven-month-old baby girl. So much swirled around her: the bustling city filled with majesty, splendor, hope, loss, love, radiance, dust, people, traffic, and so many goats. The indelible imprints made on our mind during our trip to meet Lu: our amazing daughter sleeping on her belly amidst the bustle and company of ten other babies in her nursery room; falling into the nearest rocking chair to hold her for the first time as if we were falling to our knees; feeling almost blind, deaf, and mute with overwhelming excitement and joy as we hugged her for the first time; sitting at our window and breathing the night air as we tried to listen for her cries from the courtyard in case she needed our attention; traveling to meet her birth mother, whose sacrifice, bravery, and words we will hold so closely to our hearts until it's time to share her story with Lulu; the families we met whose journeys in life converged with ours; and the warmth and protection that Lulu's nannies gave her before they placed her in our arms on that last day. Then we brought our new daughter back to a family who already loved her deeply.

The home side of our adoption is a humbling, astonishing, crazy, poignant mess of a life. Lu is now the middle child, and the only daughter of three kids ages five and under. She has seamlessly integrated into the fabric of our togetherness and our hearts. Lu was our fate and our destiny, plain and simple. She was our calling from the beginning, which we suspect traces back even further than we can comprehend. We were matched with her so many years before that fateful call—the rest was just living, believing, and connecting the dots to find her. The questions we receive about Lu's adoption range from the ridiculous ("How much does it cost to have a baby like her?"), to the fundamental, down-to-earth, and oh-so-very heartwarmingly sweet (our son Sam, age four at the time, asked, "Was I brown when I was a baby too?"), to the harrowing queries we ask ourselves every day in preparation for Lu's future. People seem to have an overwhelming sentiment of how lucky she was to be adopted or "saved." None of that's true, not for a second. As parents and children, we will likely "save" each other time and time again, as family inherently does. But as for who are the lucky ones, it's only us. We are so very, very lucky.

CASEY TRATTNER

Casey Trattner is a student at Ridgewood High School in New Jersey and enjoys singing, acting, and spending time with her parents, two brothers, sister, and friends. Her brother Yunte was adopted by her family in 2010. Casey aspires to become a history teacher or forensic anthropologist.

I thought my parents were *insane.* I have a right to be thinking all the other words in the dictionary that are defined as "parents who already have three children and want another one." You see, I'm the oldest, and therefore I often compare my life to an experimental rat in a maze. I try the maze first, and then the "scientists" (aka my parents) fix it so the next rat can get to the cheese faster. Don't get me wrong—I love my siblings, but my life was fine the way it was, and now we were going to add another kid to the mix? Um, I don't think so.

I was always the one who thought a fantastic Friday night was having friends over to watch movies instead of partying and going into town. I played life by the rules, and I was perfectly fine with that. But as we piled up paperwork and waited and waited, I found myself suddenly excited to have another rat in the lab. All my friends and family were excited too. Then, during the summer of 2010, almost two long years since my parents made the decision to adopt, we got a referral. His name was Yunte, and even though we didn't have a picture, we loved him. I loved him. The days tumbled on with going to school, complaining about homework, sleeping, complaining about school, and waiting for the time when we would meet our brother and bring him home. That moment came on December 3. Then my parents had another wacky idea, but an idea for which I was grateful. I was going to Ethiopia with them, my sister, and my brother to meet Yunte.

I had always been thankful for my lifestyle, but I'm even more thankful now. In history class (my favorite), we were learning about the French Revolution and how all the nobles and royalty would gorge themselves on lavish food, while the other 98 percent of the French were eating nothing outside the palace walls. That's how I felt eating by the hotel pool, tanning. I was afraid to go outside the hotel's protective walls for fear of what lurked out there. In fact, the only times I went outside the hotel were to go to Yunte's orphanage, the courthouse, and the museum to go see Lucy. Lucy, if you don't know, is an over-three-million-year-old hominid, the oldest relation to Homo sapiens known so far, found in Ethiopia. I had been so excited to see her until our driver, Johannes, told me she was a replica. The "real Lucy" was in a laboratory being studied in New York City, forty-five minutes from where I live.

The day we met Yunte was a day that shocked me. My mother was telling us not to be disappointed if he didn't react well to us or if he ignored us completely. We walked into the orphanage and very calmly said "hi" to my future brother. He smiled at us and threw us a ball. If I didn't love him before, I did then.

Yunte is home now and more a Trattner than we ever could have imagined. He loves to play sports (much to the delight of my sister and brother), and he loves to sing and dance (much to my liking), and we think (and hope) he likes having two older sisters and a brother. I like to think that destiny didn't bring Yunte to us but rather us to Yunte because of all the new laughter and smiles he has given us. And I realized that maybe it's not such a bad thing if my parents are insane. They wanted to share their joy and happiness with a child who wouldn't have that, and if that's not wonderfully crazy, I don't know what is. I admire my parents, and I hope one day my future husband and I will be just like them and maybe even crazier.

Yunte Trattner with his two sisters and brother

LYNNE DELUCA

*Lynne DeLuca lives in Asheville, North Carolina, and is now
retired. She lives with Terry and their dear friend Jeanne
Wright, who was instrumental in Terry's recovery. Terry is in
college preparing for a career in computer engineering.*

What I always think about most when I look back on my life with
Terry is the way I was struck by a few words from my mother. I had
never met Terry or spent much time with his mother, Michelle,
but my mom, Michelle's stepmother, always talked about what a
happy baby he was and how he always smiled. She shared with me
the troubles and challenges that Michelle and Terry had with their
very compromised health and tentative living arrangements. Michelle was fighting for her life but more so for Terry's. I knew
Michelle had a troubled past and that she had contracted AIDS.
Poor little Terry was fighting for his life because he too was in-
fected and very ill with Pneumocystis pneumonia. He was admit-
ted to the hospital at two months old, at which point Michelle
signed a DNR (Do Not Resuscitate) order. Somehow, though,
Terry pulled through it all after several months in the hospital and
many close calls with death.

While it was a miracle that Terry survived, his mother's health
continued to deteriorate, and soon it became clear that she would
not be as fortunate. One day my mom told me that Michelle had
even been interviewed by *Newsday,* with the hope that someone
would come forward to take Terry when she was gone, but no one
had responded. I could hear in my mother's voice how terribly

painful it was for her to accept that this dear, sweet little boy would have no home when his mom passed. I, on the other hand, didn't think about it. In fact, I made a concerted effort to try and push the idea of caring for him out of my head. Taking a child with AIDS in the '90s was certainly not a popular idea, and to some, it seemed dangerous.

But one day, for no apparent reason, I couldn't resist it. I knew I had to take Terry. I told my housemate that I had to do this and I called my mom and told her to tell Michelle I would take Terry if she was okay with it. My mom was so happy! She called Michelle and arranged for us to meet.

Then we went to meet him. If there had been any doubts as to whether I had made the right decision, they immediately disappeared when I saw this three-and-a-half-year-old small boy with dimples and beautiful brown eyes. My heart melted and I knew why I couldn't resist. He was entitled to a chance. He deserved an opportunity to grow up and be healthy. I couldn't let him be lost in the foster-care system.

Michelle was in the ICU at a hospital in Manhattan. At this point she could no longer talk, as she had undergone a tracheotomy because she couldn't breathe. We wrote notes, asked and answered each other's questions, and agreed that Terry would come to live with me when she passed.

Michelle died in June of 1996 and I drove to New York to pick Terry up. His future was so uncertain with regard to his health, as he was still very fragile, but I knew that I would love and care for him. Dr. Aronson, who was his pediatrician from the beginning, came to North Carolina to meet us at Duke and get us started with the right medical treatment. Over the years, Terry has faced many hurdles and scares with his battle with AIDS, and I had no idea during those times that someday we would be celebrating his graduation from high school, which we're doing this year.

Terry and his grandma still have a very special relationship. He loves her unconditionally and she adores him. He is kind, generous, open, sweet, and so bright. He's unkind to no one and loved by all. The world is a better place because he's in it.

And did I mention that he's soooo handsome!?

Terry and Dr. Jane, April 2007

KRISTIN DAVIS

*Kristin Davis is an actor, who starred as Charlotte in the HBO
series Sex in the City and recently appeared on Broadway in
The Best Man. She works on behalf of Oxfam International and
the David Sheldrick Wildlife Trust. She is the proud mother of
Gemma.*

Like so many people who adopt, I had always had a feeling that
adoption would be something I would do one day. I had a number
of professional and personal goals I wanted to accomplish first and
to have the ideal situation in place before I undertook such a major
life change. Financial security luckily fell into place, and then I
focused on whether I could do it alone.

I dreamed of the perfect partner who would love me and our
adopted child with equal measure. I waited and searched for this
partner, and time passed. Finally it became clear that I might wait
forever for the perfect partner to be available. So I decided that I
must take the leap alone. I was very anxious. I kept thinking, "Will
I be enough by myself? Will I know what to do? Will I have enough
to give to this innocent being entrusted to my care?"

The beginning was scary when my baby girl, Gemma, came
into my life. I hired wonderful help to educate myself about what
babies need. As Gemma's first year progressed, I began to realize
that I did know what to do and that I was good at caring for a baby.
This was a huge relief!

But the most important and surprising realization I have made
is that I'm not doing it alone. I *do* have the perfect partner—my

daughter, Gemma! She lets me know what she needs and she and I are the perfect team. She gives me the confidence I thought I would lack! It turns out that she gives me so much more than I could ever give her. I am so thankful that I didn't listen to my fears and took that leap.

II.

The Journey

Once the commitment to adopt is made, the real journey begins. Months of waiting for the placement of a child, whether domestic or international, can, in all truth, be torture. International adoption has increasingly been plagued with drawn-out waiting times, slow-ups, moratoriums, and closures that can cause adoptive parents to feel as if their child is trapped in their birth country. There's often fear and anxiety about the child's health issues; as kids languish in orphanages waiting for their families to get them, they can become delayed, depressed, and malnourished. Parents fear that their children will be damaged physically and emotionally forever.

I adopted twice and in both cases I felt that I might not be successful in finally getting a child because I thought I couldn't manage the paperwork. When I received the packet for my first adoption from my agency, I actually felt faint. I went home with the packet and stared at it for weeks. I went through the papers innumerable times, simply holding them in my hands, worrying that I couldn't do what was required. I was a pediatrician specializing in adoption medicine, so I shouldn't have been fazed by all the requirements! Imagine what any ordinary well-meaning person would feel.

When I decided to adopt my first son from Vietnam in 2000, I knew that I just needed to *get started* with the daunting process, so I went downtown to the Bureau of Vital Statistics to order my exemplified birth certificates. I still have no idea what "exemplified" birth certificates are, but I filled out the papers, and the birth certificates were delivered in the mail a month later. I felt like I had won the jackpot when they arrived. I also had to provide a list of all the places I had lived for the past twenty-five years, which is another daunting task faced by all potential adoptive parents. I got up very early one morning and hailed a cab to take me to the places I had lived in New York City so that I could verify all the apartment addresses. I had made a list the night before, and then I told the driver that we would be traveling all over Manhattan to confirm the addresses for my upcoming adoption. In the backseat of the taxi, I could hear him laughing as he glanced back at me in his rearview mirror. What a moment to share with a cabdriver! Successfully overcoming this one hurdle helped me to have the confidence that I would need to finish my papers and be able to adopt.

Each step I completed successfully felt like earning an "A" in school. I was proud and felt closer to my final goal. But even my excitement over such successes was dampened while waiting for the immigration clearance, which took months; there was no way of knowing when it would come. That was, without a doubt, the most annoying part of the process; everything was about waiting, and there were no guidelines, time lines, or websites to check. I realized that I had to forget about the process and just live my life.

When I adopted in 2000, there was only one woman in downtown Manhattan doing the clearance for immigration for all of New York State, and her name was Lois Troop. There was only one woman for thousands of families in New York State! It was hard to imagine, but that was the truth. When my agency finally told me that I could call Ms. Troop, I spoke to her and found out that all my papers had arrived. I just had to wait again for an immigration form called the I-171H to clear, which was another unknown. Among adoptive parents in New York, Lois Troop was legendary.

Then there's waiting for a court date abroad, which is a terrifying experience because of the instability of courts in other countries. Courts can close down temporarily, experience delays, or in some cases shut down permanently. Rumors about foreign legal situations can get out of hand, and the Internet can become a place where angry and depressed parents come together to complain. Listservs that should be about educating families and comforting them actually heighten frustrations, often creating more rumors and calamity. It's not a process that makes sense. Even the hardiest of us succumb to feelings of failure instead of feeling strong and proud about our successes. What's worse is that these feelings of failure can lead to insecurity, isolation, and depression, which doesn't help a parent get ready for a very needy baby.

Isolation can be the worst part of the journey to adopt a child. It's a very lonely process. I recall going home to my apartment in the

West Village some nights and staring blankly at the mounds of papers, with Post-it labels marking out the time line I had created. Some people get very organized and make binders with tabs, like they are students in high school. They make a calendar and track their work like they're tracking payments, grants, or contracts. I envy those people because their systems likely help them stay sane. The vast majority of people feel punished and often become angry and irritable as they wait, increasingly absorbed in the paperwork and bureaucracy of adoption as the rest of the world goes on without them. This anger and irritability are particularly acute because adoption is often a process of complete unpredictability.

There is an upside to waiting. I always encourage prospective parents to take this chance to do things that they won't do again for eighteen years, when their children are grown. To counter the frustration and isolation of paperwork and waiting around, I've always advised people in the adoption process to engage in a lot of social activities, like dinners out, theater, movies, travel, reading, or other hobbies. I also advise people to take advantage of the waiting period by creating a strategic plan for work and child care. This is an important time for people to recognize and appreciate their partnerships if they're married. I tell them to try and rediscover each other.

During the pre-adoption stage, parents should really spend time with family, especially their own parents, to help them adjust to the adoption. Friendships should be nurtured to make sure you have a support base to help you during the challenging months after the child's arrival. Sadly, some people lose friends and alienate family during the waiting period, and then there is no support when the child arrives. A tight network of family and friends is vital to an adoptive parent's adjustment to becoming a parent. A lot of work is needed, especially for those who are single or for those who are older parents. Sometimes family and friends will not give you as much support as you need or—in some cases—even understand the great desire you have to become a parent, yet it is essential to make an effort to maintain ties.

The stronger and more prepared parents are before the adoption, the better chance they have to deal well with the ups and downs of the transition period when the child first arrives. For example, I hired a nanny months before my first son arrived so that I would be prepared for his arrival. I also set up my medical practice from the time I opened it to accommodate my desire to be a full-time parent. I only worked three days a week so that I could parent the other four. I created a schedule for myself so that I was free in the mornings for the first six weeks of Ben's preschool program to help him transition to school. On top of all that, I made rules about my night commitments once Ben arrived so that I was never out at night more than once a week. My day started later so that I could give him breakfast and play with him before I left for work.

Once you finally arrive in the country where your child was born to bring her home, so much can happen that will exhaust, confuse, and delight you. Moments of wonder and amazement are common when parents meet family members of the adoptee or make friends at the orphanage. Families are frequently moved by emotional encounters with caring foster parents who deeply love their child. Sweet and tender tales are told about how foster parents cry when the child is physically handed to the adoptive parents. Holding a Giving and Receiving Ceremony with the individuals who have cared for your child can be a moving experience and a story that your child will hold dear all his life. My son Ben loves to tell the story of how he vomited all over Dr. Vinh, the orphanage director, at his Giving and Receiving Ceremony in Hanoi.

Suddenly we are parents, and we don't know much and we are unprepared. We are expected to be wise, as if we were born to be parents. After parenting two sons, now twelve and fourteen, and practicing thirty years as a pediatrician, I conclude that there should be more preparation for parenting, whether it is through the old-fashioned way or adoption. That preparation should be life-long. Parenting lasts decades. Maybe it never ends!

As parents, we ask a lot of questions about who our children will be, and we fantasize about their future. We dream of them growing up and reaching the milestones of walking, talking, self-feeding, toilet training, and going to school for the first time. When you give birth to a baby, you feel a sense of control that is likely not based on much science. Simply because the baby comes from your body and has your genes, you are certain that you can control and predict the final outcome. I don't think that this is true, but what I have observed about parents who adopt is that they feel they have almost no control. They imagine that because the birth parents are mostly unknown, especially in international adoption, they are in a "blind" process. In particular, the process to adopt from Ukraine and Russia can be completely blind until you travel there to meet the child for the first time. In the adoption medicine world, we often speak about the "leap of faith" required when creating a family. The stories that follow beautifully capture this leap of faith.

CLAUDE KNOBLER

Claude Knobler lives in Los Angeles with his wife, Mary Knobler, three children, dog, cat, and fish. He is generally very tired.

In the end, it was my wife who made me meet my son's mother.

Mary and I had decided to adopt a child from Ethiopia and had, along with our kids, Clay and Grace, somehow found a beautiful five-year-old boy named Nati. His father was dead, but his mother, though sick with AIDS, was still alive. Unable to take care of her son, she'd placed him in an orphanage for adoption six months before.

When we were told I could meet Nati's mother when I went to Africa to pick up our son, my wife prepared a list of questions for me to ask about Nati's medical history, his relationship with his birth father, and his general upbringing. I was instructed to ask for baby stories, favorite foods, general likes and dislikes, and as much of Nati's genealogy as I could gather.

I, in turn, told my wife that I would really rather, you know, *not*.

I was, sad to say, terrified that meeting Nati's mother would be too hard . . . for me, if not for Nati.

To my credit, I did at least realize that I never stood a chance of winning that argument.

A few days after I arrived in Africa, a woman at Nati's orphanage arranged for me to meet my son's mother. On the day of our meeting I was more scared than I'd ever been in my life.

And then I saw her.

We got out of the car and Nati's mother hugged him. It occurred to me that this moment was going to be the last time I would not be responsible for Nati, the last time he would not fully be my own child. And all of the questions I was prepared to ask about Nati—and all of my fears—vanished. I wasn't there to learn anything. I wasn't there for Nati. I was there to watch a mother say good-bye to her son, and that was it.

Her eyes were red from tears and yellow from illness. Nati sat on his mother's lap and she stroked his head. After a while, I asked Nati's mother if she'd mind if I took some photos for Nati. "These are photos your son will look at after you're gone," I thought to myself. These are his memories of you for when he lives far away from here. I felt as if I were doing something cold and cruel. I watched as Nati's mother said good-bye. She spoke softly into his ear, as though she could imprint a memory of herself into him through sheer whispered will.

I took out some pictures of Mary, Clay, Grace, and our home. I tried to find the perfect words, though everything I said was being translated. I avoided saying that Clay was "my son," not wanting her to think that I didn't consider Nati to be the same as a son, and yet not wanting her to think that I did either. "This is Clay; he'll be Nati's brother," I said. "This is Gracie." "This is where Nati will go to school." "This is our home." Nati, on the other hand, was gleeful. He and I had looked at all of the pictures; we'd used them as flash cards for him to learn the members of his new family.

"American mom!" he shouted out when we came to a photo of Mary.

I cringed and tried to hide it.

After half an hour, Nati's aunt, a polite but somewhat distant woman who was unable to care for Nati herself, asked if I would come back the next day so that other family members could come and say good-bye.

That night I spoke to Mary and told her about meeting Nati's mother. Nati and I had some dinner, watched TV, and then I put him to bed. The next day, we arrived at the same restaurant but were met by a much larger group. I sat down and tried to slip into the background. Nati sat on his mother's lap. He looked bored—the way kids do when they're stuck at a table filled with grown-ups.

I sat next to Nati's cousin and asked a few questions. I learned that Nati's mother and father had eloped, and that his father had liked practical jokes, spent time as a soldier, and contracted AIDS after getting a bad blood transfusion following a car accident. As he lay dying, he wrote the words "I love Nati" all over the wall near his bed. Nati was only a year and a half old.

I drew a bit closer to Nati's mother. Through our translator, I told her that my wife would want me to say that we would take good care of her son. That he would have a great school and a nice home. She nodded, but the words all seemed like dust coming out of my mouth. This woman, with her tired, pained eyes, had decided long ago to give up her son so that he could have all of those things, but now, none of them mattered. She was saying good-bye. I was a distraction and nothing else.

Nati's mother didn't cry when we left. He and I got into our car and I told him to wave good-bye to his family. They stood there in the dirt parking lot of a restaurant in Addis Ababa and watched us go.

We got back to our hotel, and while I packed a few things, Nati sat quietly and then began to cry. He was hungry, he told me. He was tired. He didn't know what he wanted to eat. Then I asked if he wanted to go downstairs to the lobby for a soda. We sat together, father and son, in the lobby and shared a 7-Up. Then we went back to the room. When we returned to the lobby an hour later to check out, our waitress ran to us. I had forgotten to pay the bill. Anxious to show her that I was an idiot and not a crook, I apologized profusely.

"I'm soooo sorry," I said. "I'm soooo sorry." I gave her far too much money and told her to keep it.

Then Nati turned to me and began to laugh.

"I'm soooo sorry," he said, imitating me. "I'm sooooo sorry."

He laughed some more. Then the woman behind the checkout desk laughed and so did I. Nati kept at it, and the words "I'm soooo sorry" became our shared joke. We say it to each other sometimes still, when one of us has done something to annoy the other.

"I'm soooo sorry," Nati will say with a big smile when I scold him for shouting in the house.

"I'm soooo sorry," I'll tell him when he gets annoyed at me for tickling him while he's trying to watch TV.

Claude and Nati Knobler

"I'm soooo sorry," we'll tell each other here in his new home, far away from the place he was born.

When I think now of Nati's mother, I don't think of her sacrifice, or her bravery, or even the love she so clearly had for her boy, my boy, our boy. Instead I think only of her eyes, the saddest ones I have ever seen.

I am so sorry.

DARCI PICOULT

Darci Picoult is a playwright, screenwriter, and essayist whose
work has been produced nationally. She lives in Brooklyn,
New York, with her husband and two daughters, adopted from
China in 1998 and 2002.

A TRUE CONCEPTION

Maya, age five, hands me an anniversary gift along with a question. Her family has joined me and my husband, Larry, for dinner. She places a candle in my palm and looks up at me.

"Darci, did all of your children die?"

I swallow hard and look at Maya's father for help. He is busy feeding her baby brother. Her mother is talking to Larry.

"Did they?" she asks again.

"No, Maya. I haven't had children yet."

She looks at me, confused, and twirls a noodle into her mouth.

"But Larry and I are going to adopt a baby from China."

Her face lights up. "Is Larry Chinese?"

When I was ten years old, I read *The Good Earth* by Pearl S. Buck and fantasized about adopting a baby from China. One night, I snuck into my mom's makeup and extended my eyes with thick black eyeliner. I sleeked back my curls with Dippity-do, slid into one of her dresses, tiptoed outside, and rang the doorbell. When my mom opened the door, she was greeted by my cry, "I want my daughter!"

In seven or eight months, Larry and I will receive a referral of our daughter from China. We will be given her name, picture, medical records, and any other information on her from the orphanage. We will not know who her birth parents are or why they chose not to raise her. We are told that China's one child per family rule creates a preference for sons. We are also told that my infertility is due to my DES exposure. But in truth we will never know the exact reason we were brought together with our daughter.

"A true conception" is what my friend Liz calls it. She adopted her daughter, Hana, from China in 1995 and has become my guidance counselor during this process. "Get five original copies of everything," she advised, as we began to gather our required documents. Within a few months, our ability to parent was scrutinized by state and federal bureaucrats and our life was divided into folders marked "Fingerprints," "Finances," "Medical History," "Addresses since 1975/Sexual Abuse Clearance." I wonder if all people wanting children should be required to do this.

But this pregnancy defies the norm. This pregnancy will never show itself to the outside world, but inside there is a swelling of anticipation. Even my husband can feel her kick. One night, he lay awake in bed. "We should send a prayer to her parents," he said. "Maybe she was just conceived." Each night since, as I shut my eyes in prayer, I picture her tiny body with wonder. What will her fingers look like? And her legs? Will they be long or short? Does she lie curled in a womb or in an orphanage bed? Night after night, these questions divide and multiply, growing large in my head. Is she hungry? Is she held? How often? By whom? Does she long for me as I do for her? "Faith," Larry whispers. "We must have faith."

Faith implants itself within me and begins to gestate. I know that anytime a child is brought into this world, there are no guarantees. But there are gynecological visits, amniocentesis tests, and prenatal vitamins that help ensure a healthy delivery. Our daughter's delivery will have its own safety measures provided by our adoption agency and government authorities in both the United States and China. But ultimately, who she is and when she is delivered are in the hands of foreign officials whom we will never meet. They will read our numerous documents and select our child accordingly. How they know which baby goes with which parent is an equation that I cannot fathom, for this conception goes beyond reason. This conception stems from a yearning and a desire to love that transcends my mind and overtakes my heart.

The day our documents receive their final blessings before being sent to China, I can hardly control myself. "I'm going to be a mother." The words jump out of my mouth and land on any ears that are in close proximity, like those of the lady behind the copy machine, the notary, and the police officer who processes my record. Complete strangers have become midwives in the birth of my child. When they slap the bottom of our documents with their seals and stamps, I can hear her cry.

CAROLYN JACOBS

Carolyn is a writer/producer and cofounder of Read It All Up,
a new business focused on the joy of reading and eating. She
lives with her son up the river from New York City.

When I got on the plane to go to Vietnam to bring home my son, I was nowhere near ready to be a mom. Sure, I was schlepping around a giant duffel bag filled with forty pounds of diapers, formula, pj's, toys, medical supplies, snacks, and books like *The Birth of a Mother* and *Dr. Spock's Baby and Child Care.* I had just been through a year and a half of grueling interviews, applications, background checks, paperwork for government officials, and financial scrutiny that exceeded even that of the IRS. In those final moments at the airport, I was convinced the friends who wrote my references and all the strangers who finally stamped me with approval to adopt an eleven-month-old boy had made a mistake. Somehow I had bamboozled them. For that matter, I had bamboozled myself. Longing to be a mom didn't outweigh actual training. I had begun to feel a terror since turning forty-five, a fear that old age without the right man might be sad and that going without having loved and raised a child would be unendurable. These feelings were now a mere blip in my gut next to the panic I felt as I moved step-by-step toward the plane.

Years before I decided to adopt, I had a dream that I was in a dark and scary forest with a little boy holding my hand. We suddenly emerged from the woods to see the edge of the earth and the moon, a giant stone ball with every crater visible, filling the sky.

The moon was moving toward us, closer and closer with the speed of inevitability. I knew there was no safe place to go, but nonetheless, I snatched up the boy, who was mine and yet not mine, and started to run.

Now, as I prepared to fly to Vietnam, I knew where we were running to: Pacific Airways Flight 27, and the destination was the far side of that moon.

As I heaved the overweight duffel bag onto the scale, it occurred to me that this was my very last chance to change my mind. And I might have, but I had my son's picture tucked inside the passport strapped to my belly. That little face with the big dark eyes looking at me with bold curiosity instead of fear was a face that was strangely familiar already. I swore I had done an etching of a boy with that exact curve of cheek for a college art class in my twenties. I took a picture of a boy with an identically dimpled grin, both tentative and sly, when I worked on a movie in China in my thirties. It hung on the wall of my kitchen and made me smile every morning for years.

When Dr. Jane looked at my son's adoption referral picture, she instantly declared him a "juicy boy," and she was right. I packed a medical kit per her meticulous instructions down to the last cotton ball that was my talisman and safety net. I used every single item on her list, from the nebulizer with the duckbill-shaped mouthpiece to the scabies cream and the baby Benadryl. When Luc-Thinh (then named Quang Thinh) had a cough, I took him into the hotel bathroom and blasted hot water from the shower for steam, exactly as her notes instructed. I just didn't have the common sense to remove his pj's beforehand, and within minutes I had a screaming child covered in welts. By the time our taxi reached the English-speaking health clinic near the hotel, Luc was asleep in my arms. His skin was back to normal, but at that point the doctor visit was for both of us.

The clinic pediatrician was named Lucien and he looked like Dr. Kildare. At another time I might have cared that there was spit-up on my sweater and grease on my nose, but that night it only mattered that Luc-Thinh was examined inch by inch with delicate scrutiny and pronounced healthy. Needless to say, during the two weeks we stayed in Hanoi, we were regulars at that clinic and on a first-name basis with the staff. They sized me up as the type to run in for every bump, scrape, or wheeze. They didn't know the half of it. I checked Luc's breathing even when he was awake. I just wanted to be safe and not sorry. It was only right; look what I was protecting! This tiny boy had so much courage already. He had been torn from everything he knew but still staggered around like a drunken pirate grabbing at the sights and sounds of his new life. There was a sassy tilt to his chin demanding, "So *nu*?" Best of all, he didn't seem to mind the white-skinned Jewish lady with crazy gray hair chirping "I love you" over and over in bad Vietnamese. I prayed I wouldn't run out of Cheerios. I prayed he would survive all my mistakes. That's all I asked.

Now that Luc-Thinh is five, of course I ask considerably more. I ask that it be sunny for Saturday soccer, and that he won't be too scared when he boards "the big boy bus" to go to his first day of kindergarten. I ask that he won't get sick on days I have shoots or meetings that might lead to more work. I ask forgiveness for letting him watch the music video *Thriller*, with its werewolves and dancing ghouls. I ask for advice and inspiration from friends about how to transform an appalling lapse of judgment into a useful lesson. I ask that Luc will always keep that bop in his step, and that we'll never forget his buddy, a stuffed toy he named Crispy Crab, whenever we leave the house. Mostly I ask that he won't grow up too fast; this time of the big moon is so precious. The other day he looked up at me from the bathtub and promised, "Don't worry, Mommy. I'm not in a rush."

That's a relief, because I'm not nearly ready.

Luc-Thinh Jacobs

SHONDA RHIMES

Shonda Rhimes is the creator of the television shows Grey's Anatomy *and* Private Practice. *She lives in Los Angeles with her two daughters.*

SURRENDER

I am sitting in a parking garage inside a rental car in Detroit, Michigan. The car is not moving, but my hands are gripping the wheel like I'm in a high-speed chase. Mary J. Blige is singing "No More Drama" on the radio, and from now on, whenever anyone mentions Detroit, this song will pop into my head. It is June 2002. At this moment, four floors away, inside an operating room, my daughter is being born.

I am sitting in my car in Los Angeles, California. My mind is racing, the car sits running but still stuck in rush-hour traffic. Frank Sinatra is singing on the radio, but I don't notice because I am too busy shouting questions into my cell phone. It is February 2012. At this moment, two states away, my daughter is being born.

I've never been in a delivery room. I've never pushed. My water has never broken—hell, I've never had any water to break. My friends talk about the horrors of pregnancy—hemorrhoids and episiotomies and that awful moment when, in the midst of pushing, they poop on the table. They tell me about their special organic pregnancy diets and how, as they grow life inside them, they avoid coffee and alcohol and people who smoke. I listen to them, intrigued in a detached way. I'm happy for them, but I feel no pangs of "I wish that were me." I feel no jealousy.

I've never wanted to be pregnant, never suffered through the infertility that devastates some of my friends. Since I was nine years old, I've been telling people that, when I have children, I will adopt. It's always been a fact for me. I don't know why. I think when I was younger the idea seemed bold to me and slightly defiant—why it is just *lazy* to *make* people when there were so many people out there who need mothers! Like I said, I was young. As I got older, the idea matured too. It took shape and form and became real. Adoption was how I was going to become a mother. Adoption would build my family.

Looking at the process of adoption, it makes sense how comfortable I was with it. I'm a former straight-"A" student. I am driven and I like goals. I am a list maker and nothing makes my mind hum at a better frequency than huge quantities of research to complete. When you are planning to adopt, you spend months researching—domestic, international, agency, private, foster, open, closed, older child, newborn, special needs. You become well versed in a new lingo—interstate compact, service provider, decrees. There are mountains of paperwork—financial statements, personal essays, biographies, medical reports. You get fingerprinted and photographed and interviewed and examined . . . and then a birth mother picks you. You get picked. Your hard work pays off. Let me tell you, the annoying teenage girl who likes to raise her hand first in class still lives inside me and she was euphoric.

I didn't count on what happens after that. After all that paperwork, all that control, I didn't count on the need to face what it means to surrender.

I was chosen. The first time in 2002, I was chosen by a birth mother to raise her child. I was shown beautiful fuzzy ultrasound photos. I flew to Detroit and met a woman who was pregnant, alone, and in crisis. Back at home, I spoke to my daughter's birth mother on the phone every single evening. We discussed our favorite television shows and trashy mystery novels. She told me stories from her childhood, stories that made my skin crawl because it horrified me that life should be that difficult for a child. She told me things that made me love her resilience. And she had a wild sense of humor—we made ourselves sick with laughter over the silliest things. We became friends. We never talked about the baby growing in her belly.

Never.

Ever.

Not once.

I had questions. I had type-A hand-raised-in-class intense questions. Did she eat vegetables? Why hadn't she had any early medical care? Could she feel the baby moving? Did she read to the baby? Had she REALLY stopped drinking once she knew she was pregnant?

I did not ask. I kept my questions to myself. It was driving me insane, but I knew to leave her be. I knew I had no control. I had read all the books and I had talked to other parents who'd adopted. Surrender, they told me. You have to just let go and accept that you have no control and surrender to the process, one friend said as she buckled her daughter into her car seat. She'd adopted three times from two different countries. *Surrender, Shonda. Surrender.*

In 2012, it was the adoption agency that chose me. The birth mother was a woman I never had the honor to meet. She didn't want to know me. I imagined her wrapped in a tight blanket of pain, unable to deal with the reality of another mother. My heart broke for her on a daily basis. But I spent her pregnancy acting like a dog locked out of the house and constantly searching for a way in.

"Does she want pictures of me?" No.

"Can I have pictures of her?" No.

"Should I write her a letter?" No.

"Does she want to write a letter to the baby?" Maybe.

"Can I send her anything?" No.

"Does anyone know what her favorite color is?" No.

"Her hobbies?" She's athletic.

"Oh, does she play soccer or volleyball or basketball or swim or dance or . . . ?" She is just athletic.

"What does that mean!?"

My hand was raised and no one was calling on me. Once again, I had no control. I never learned what "athletic" meant. I never learned her favorite color. I never met her. By her own choice, she was a mystery. *Surrender, Shonda. Just . . . surrender.*

One birth mother I knew and one I didn't. One was middle class, one was poor. One was in her thirties and one was barely in her twenties. But the situations were, oddly, exactly the same. There were babies growing in bellies and it didn't have a thing to do with me. They weren't my babies yet. I loved them and I loved their birth mothers and I decorated nurseries and bought baby clothes and came up with names, and all the while, running through my mind in a continuous loop, was the reminder that anything could happen. That I needed to surrender to the process. That birth mothers change their minds. And honestly, I support the idea of birth mothers changing their minds. I support the idea of a birth mother keeping her child if she can. I do. But I was still climbing the imaginary walls of my mind. I had no control. *Surrender to the process, surrender to the process, surrender to the process. . . .*

So there I am in 2002. Sitting in the parking garage in Michigan while my daughter is being born. It's an emergency C-section and the birth mom was given a choice of who she wanted to go to the operating room with. I stood there, all hopeful and excited and ready to gown up. But she chose her sister-in-law. I'd choose my family member too instead of the intense, tightly wound ball of nerves that was me. Anyone would. But after the nurses and orderlies rolled her out to head to the operating room, I stood alone in that room and I knew I was going to cry. I'm not a crier. I don't like to cry in public. I don't like to cry in private. I like to think that I inherited my mother's Southern black woman stoicism. But that stoicism was in danger. Which is how I ended up in the parking garage listening to Mary J. Blige, my hands gripping the steering wheel so hard that I'd have marks on my palms for several days.

It was in that car that I finally understood the surrender. That I finally fully accepted that this wasn't my process. That something in me broke open. Because I realized that I wasn't sitting in that car thinking about me. I was sitting in that car thinking about the scared girl heading for an operating room having a baby she would ultimately hand over. To me. This wasn't my surrender. It was hers.

I cried more in that car than I have in a long time.

Ten years later, the whole process is like a long-unused muscle for me. But I exercise it as best as I can. I try to stop asking questions. I try to stop lying awake at night worrying. I look at the ultrasound photo five thousand times a day and I breathe and I try to refrain from raising my hand at all. I let go of any sense of control and I tell people that anything can happen. That maybe I have a baby. But mostly I think of the birth mother, who doesn't want to meet me. How scared she must be. How alone she must feel. What a leap of faith she is taking. She is preparing to send her tiny daughter out into the world with the hope that all will be well. I filled out papers and wrote letters and got a home study and I hoped and I dreamed, but she is doing all the work. She is surrendering a piece of her soul to the universe and hoping for the best. I don't have to meet her to know that.

I've never been in a delivery room. I've never pushed. I've never had any water to break. I can't discuss hemorrhoids or episiotomies or pooping on the table. But I am a mother.

In 2012, my daughter's birth mother stayed in the hospital after delivery just long enough to make sure that I had arrived. Then she did the hardest thing imaginable. She got dressed and she left the hospital without her baby. I was told that, before she left, she asked if I was there. Yes, they told her. I was told she asked if I loved the baby.

Yes. Yes, I did.

Yes, I do.

SARAH EDWARDS-SCHMIDT

*Sarah is a development officer for a national nonprofit
environmental organization headquartered in New York City.
She lives in Brooklyn with her husband, son, and stepdaughter.*

In 2007, my husband and I adopted our amazing son, Milo, from
Kazakhstan, a country where prospective parents usually make
two separate trips, spaced about a month apart, to complete the
adoption process. Our first visit to his baby house in Astana, Kazakhstan's capital, located in the steppes near the country's boom-
ing oil fields, was in February, during the icy depths of winter.
Over the course of nearly a month of daily "bonding" visits, we fell
massively in love with our son, who at eight months old already
exhibited the charisma and sociability that are the hallmarks of his
personality to this day. All adoptive parents who've done their
homework know about the huge importance of attachment, and as
we played with Milo in the warmth of the baby house each day, we
felt sure that we were starting to build a strong bond.

When it came time to say our temporary good-byes and return
to the United States in between trips, however, I was bereft. I felt
guilty that we were leaving Milo behind just when he was getting
to know and trust us. I worried that he would forget us, or worse,
that he would remember our temporary abandonment all too viv-
idly, which would create attachment problems moving forward.
My husband had a much more sanguine approach, pointing out
that Milo had survived his first eight months without us, that he
seemed an inherently happy kid, and that one month apart wasn't

a big deal in the cosmic scheme of things. Logically I knew he was right, but emotionally I remained convinced that the underpinnings of this precious new relationship would be completely demolished by our time away, and that thought broke my heart. Back in New York, my emotions were further inflamed every time I read a memory book filled with messages to Milo written by the women who took care of him in "Group Kiddy" at the baby house. Missing Milo terribly, I would get in bed every night and sob as I read their loving wishes for his future, which seemed even sweeter in the sometimes awkward translation from Russian to English: "Be a cheerful butterfly." "I wish your angel never leaves you." "I send you the ocean of smiles." "Be big and strong boy." It got to the point where my husband threatened to hide the book because it got me so worked up.

The time in between trips felt like the longest month ever. When it came time to return to Kazakhstan, I was beyond excited. I felt in control and back on track, confident that in less than twenty-four hours we would be reunited with Milo to begin our real life as a family. As luck would have it, a major snowstorm hit the East Coast the night of our departure. We were stuck at Newark airport with a long flight delay, causing us to miss our connecting flight in Frankfurt, one of the few each week that flew directly to Astana. I was anxiety stricken, sure that we'd have to wait days to get there, and fearing that somehow the very adoption itself would be threatened if we didn't arrive *exactly* as planned. Figuring out how we would get back to our son felt like an insurmountable problem, and for the first time in our entire adoption process, I lost hope.

As it turned out, my admittedly completely overdramatic and

control-freakish moment of despair provided a great window into the challenges of parenting. It was a vivid reminder that we have little control in life, other than in the way we choose to go about tackling problems. It is the grace and good humor we can bring to the process that saves us. My husband and I had already learned that lesson in dealing with infertility and in our pursuit of international adoption, but in the rush of it all, I had forgotten.

The very helpful Lufthansa staff in Frankfurt figured out that if we flew to Istanbul the next morning, we could arrive in Astana only one day later than originally planned. To top it off, they offered to foot the bill for our hotel and dinner for the night. Expecting the German equivalent of a Motel 6 and McDonald's, we were delighted when our taxi took us half an hour out of town to a historic country hotel, where we enjoyed an impromptu pre-Milo "date night" complete with a candlelit dinner in the courtyard of a picturesque old stable. A full night's sleep in such lovely surroundings restored my equilibrium and left us refreshed and ready to enjoy every bit of the big adventures ahead. We spent hours exploring the Istanbul airport with great Turkish food and fantastic souvenir shopping. We were surrounded by rough-and-tumble oil field workers during our flight from Istanbul to Astana. I seemed to be the only woman other than our flight attendants, who were kept busy doling out copious amounts of vodka to the rowdy passengers. We had an only slightly delayed reunion with our son, who cracked the best smile in the history of smiling when he saw us walk into his room at the baby house. His caregivers put him in our arms and told us how much he had missed his new parents. Everyone cried as we said good-bye, except for Milo, who was surrounded by so much love that he was more than fine.

Of course, this happy ending was just a beginning, as making it "through" the adoption itself was just the start of our family adventures. As he fills our lives with joy, Milo reminds us each and every day how important it is to stay strong, never lose heart, go with the flow, embrace the chaos, and most of all, sit back and enjoy every moment of the ride.

WENDY LIPP

Wendy Lipp is a stay-at-home mom. She resides in Pound Ridge, New York, with husband, Fulvio Segalla, and children Yabi, Luca, and Jesse.

The road you leave behind,
Ahead lies mystery.

—STEVIE WONDER

I had a coffee and a Danish at the JFK terminal on July 2, 2005. I bought, read, and discarded a *People* magazine. I looked around and drummed my fingers expectantly. I felt butterflies flitting around in my stomach about every thirty seconds.

When my husband showed up with Yaebsira, our brand-new, eleven-month-old baby boy from Ethiopia, my chorus sang. I knew that when he put the baby into my arms, the baby and I would make eye contact and understand our mutual bond, just as it was with my two biological children. When it actually happened, Yabi placed his hands on each of my shoulders, shifted his weight, and craned his body and neck away from me to look all around the room over my head. Moments later, I sat down with him in my lap and began to trace my fingers on his small hand. He wouldn't let me touch his open palm. I thought, "Hmmmmmm . . ."

Now my boy is six. He is lovely and hilarious. He wears a crown of obstinacy; he is a young, contrarian prince in Old Navy jeans. We hold hands often. He teaches me that I have as much to learn as he. He taught me to crack my heart open to whoever came through that door at JFK. And why not? We humans are always cracking our hearts open all the time anyway. And we never know what babies will bring, whether they are homegrown, handpicked, or arranged for scientifically. As we like to say, it's all good.

I am as in love and obsessed with Yabi as I am with my other two children. They are my three children, thank goodness. And I'm not taking nothin'—not one livin' moment—for granted.

Yaebsira Robert Segalla ("Yabi")

ELLEN AND LOUIS PAFFUMI

The Paffumi family lives in Guilford, Connecticut. Ellen and Louis's daughter, Olivia Rose, was adopted from Vinh Phúc, Vietnam, in October 2001.

Just as we were leaving for the airport, Dr. Jane phoned with the advice to relax and enjoy the flight because this would be our last time together as a couple without a child. What a wise woman. So we tried that for a while.

It's been ten years and I can still remember the humidity in the air and the anxiety we felt as we quickly and chaotically made our way from the Hanoi airport north to the orphanage in Vinh Phúc. We were being driven directly there after our twenty-plus-hour flight from New York because the local provincial officials were going to be unavailable for several weeks. The adoption agency had decided to squeeze our Giving and Receiving Ceremony in before the officials departed. It was our first time in Vietnam and we were traveling alone, so it was quite a culture shock. The heat, the poverty, and the rural roads filled with masses of people carrying all their worldly possessions on motorbikes were new to us. The frantic pace at which everybody moved was so foreign and seemed so disorganized.

We were dressed in the clothes that we had tossed into our carry-on bags at the last minute "just in case" we needed them. We had changed in the plane lavatory. The "just in case" had happened because our luggage was lost in Hong Kong. In that lost luggage were the necessary baby paraphernalia that we had so carefully purchased and packed for months, as well as gifts for the orphanage children and staff. As we drove along, dodging motorbikes and water buffaloes, I kept wondering and panicking about how this was going to work. After all the meticulous planning and all the tedious paperwork, how on earth would we ever find and be able to bring our baby girl home in the middle of all this chaos? What would we do without diapers and formula?

We did find and meet our daughter. Of course the driver managed to navigate his way through the traffic, and later that same day, we arrived at the orphanage, where all the chaos and noise seemed to melt away. I will always remember the first time I saw our daughter's beautiful huge black eyes. We named her Olivia because her eyes were like olives. She was staring and smiling at us and looked like she had been patiently waiting for us. We spent several hours with the wonderful staff at the orphanage, not understanding a word they were saying (our translator had disappeared and then reappeared when it was time to go) but communicating perfectly. We were getting to know our daughter and appreciating the goodness of these people; they were kind enough to go out and buy us diapers and formula.

We brought our daughter, Olivia Rose Luc Thi Nam, home to the United States. It has been ten years since then, and she is a young lady who is very proud of who she is and her Vietnamese heritage. When I look back at all the paperwork, home studies, waiting, travel, humidity, and lost luggage, and the delay by U.S. Customs (which is another story . . .), I would do it again in a heartbeat. At the time, it was so stressful, but the experience of traveling to Olivia Rose's birth country was such an important part of the process of becoming her family .

And our luggage arrived from Hong Kong too. Happy ending.

HEATHER HAGGERTY WOOLSLAYER AND DONALD WOOLSLAYER

Heather is a stay-at-home mom of three wonderful Chinese daughters. She resides in Mays Landing, New Jersey, with Grace, Banyan, Lyla, and her husband, Don.

Grace means a gift from God, and my husband, Don, and I spent over ten years praying for the graces to be patient as we waited and tried to start a family. Once we determined that adoption would be our path to a family, we were at peace. We chose China, or maybe China chose us, for two reasons in particular: first, we wanted to support the women of China who are pressured to give up their baby girls (one-child family policy), and second, the process of adoption from China had a great reputation—fast and stable. So we waited, dreamed, and planned.

After the usual grunt and grind of paperwork and waiting, we got the call. We went to China filled with excitement and great joy, but that was short-lived. Sophie, our beautiful new baby, seemed okay the first day or two, but then she began to get very sick. She was despondent, listless, and unable to keep any food down. At first we thought she might be sick due to the stress and anxiety of being with new people in a new environment. As days passed, we worked with our doctor and waited desperately for the trip home, but Sophie became more and more fragile and never made it. She passed away on the morning of the eighth day of our time in China. Besides the shock, sadness, and disbelief, the journey wasn't over.

We were so scared and perplexed. What happened? Why did she die? We requested an autopsy, but there were no answers. We met with orphanage administrators, doctors, American consulate officials, and we had many conversations with our adoption agency. After almost a month in China we came home with no answers, with our daughter's remains, and had a funeral and burial for her. It may seem pretty black-and-white, but it actually wasn't.

The entire trip was filled with many unexpected graces. After Sophie passed away, while we were still in China, we had meetings with Chinese officials in which it was hinted that they might never let us adopt another little girl. Because there was no clear cause of death established, there may have been a distrust of us as parents. We were able to finally understand this conclusion, but Don and I kept our faith that we would be able to adopt eventually. Our friends and family pleaded with us to come home, but a few adoption facilitators in China advised us to stay to see if we could adopt another child right then, and we agreed. This did not happen, however, and in the long run, it was a blessing.

Once we returned home to the United States and settled in, we found another adoption agency and began the adoption process over again. They were our guardian angels. China Center of Adoption Affairs (CCAA) invited us to adopt. The fact that I went back was a grace in itself! We were gun-shy and feared that we would never have a family, but we were on our way, and that's where the graces sealed the deal.

I had just finished my school year teaching, and Don had agreed to go on a retreat with me and my therapist and a group of other patients. I really needed some healing and acceptance of myself. So we left on a Thursday afternoon in June, looking forward to some time away together.

On the car ride, Don whipped out a U2 CD and said, "I want you to listen to this song."

I said, "Okay," of course.

It was called "Grace." It talked about wiping away the stain and accepting everyone and really forgiving. It sounded like our story. Don said he would like to name our daughter, if and when we got the call, Grace. I wasn't as enthused, because I thought the name was not unique enough (typical me). As soon as we arrived at the retreat, I looked down the row of people we were going to be spending the weekend with, and there was this woman who looked a great deal like my own aunt Grace; this was very weird! At the closing of the weekend, we were on top of a hill listening to music and "Amazing Grace" started playing. Then on the way home in the car, I had a terrible headache and I was in the passenger seat with my eyes closed. I opened them at one point to see a license plate in front of us that said GR8 GIFT, which is "grace." I was getting the message.

As soon as we arrived home, we went out to dinner for our wedding anniversary. It wasn't until the next day that I checked our messages and learned that while we were gone our agency was trying to get in touch with us. I called Don at work and told him that Grace was ours and waiting for us in China.

The graces have continued to flow. Our daughter has brought peace and fulfillment and all the graces we needed to heal. Our third adoption was a girl named Banyan, and just like the tree that is her namesake, she adds a strong new branch to our family. And our fourth adoption, which was just completed in April 2011, is our daughter Lyla Jayne, whose name reflects the many important "Janes" who have blessed our lives.

The power of God's gift of grace allowed Don and I to keep our hearts open to the possibility of a family. It is through these graces that we have the treasures of our hearts, Sophie, Grace, Banyan, and Lyla.

PAT LOCKE

Patricia is a corporate communications executive in New York. She lives in Brooklyn with her son, Victor, and their Shih Tzu pup, Buddy.

A leap of faith. Was I ready to take it? All we had were a handful of blurry photographs and a two-minute videotape. After six years of fertility treatments, including two in-vitro procedures, mountains of paperwork, and a trip to a corner of Eastern Europe that I had never heard of, we were about to meet our son. Would I fall in love with him immediately? Would I even feel anything at all? Would he cry when I held him? Would I know what to do?

I wasn't at my best. I didn't sleep the night before, and it wasn't because I was anxious about meeting the sad-faced little boy I had seen in the pictures the adoption agency had sent us. My husband and I had been up all night, dealing with the agonizing realization that our marriage was coming apart. Right at the moment when we should be the happiest, we were the most miserable. We kept asking ourselves, should we go through with this, knowing that we might not be together to raise our new son?

We traveled in silence to the orphanage. It was wintertime, and we'd heard that the heat in the orphanage would regularly go off because the government couldn't pay its bills. The facilities were poor but clean, and the caretakers were pleasant and efficient, if not overly warm. We sat there, holding our feelings at bay, waiting for the attendant to bring him in. And then, there he was. He was small and pale, with a red nose and cold fingers, wearing a little white babushka and a blue *101 Dalmatians* jumper. His name was Victor, and we decided from the start that he would keep it because it was the only thing he had that was his. He didn't cry when I put him on my lap, but he didn't seem especially glad to see me either. He did like the Cheerios I brought, and the toys, especially a set of colored nesting cups. We sat and played for a while until the attendant took him away. I was charmed, and the seeds of what would eventually grow into deep, unconditional love were planted.

Then it was off to court to swear to the stern-faced judge that we had the means to care for him, which is what the officials were really concerned about. After answering some questions and signing more papers, it was over. Victor was ours, but we couldn't take him home just yet. We went back to the orphanage the next day to see him one more time, and we left behind some pictures and a cuddly toy before going home for the monthlong waiting period the government takes to process all of the paperwork.

The next three weeks were surreal, filled with a flurry of painting and preparing for our little boy's arrival, combined with long and difficult discussions about our relationship. Not exactly the way I had dreamed it all would be. But I was determined that Victor would have a good life with us, whether we stayed together or not.

When we returned to pick him up, the air was warmer and filled with the first signs of spring. Our spirits were brighter too; my husband and I had called a truce and decided to give it all we had to keep our marriage together. I remember changing Victor out of his orphanage clothes and dressing him in one of the brand-new outfits I had so much fun shopping for during the waiting period. As I looked around at the other children and the caretakers with whom he'd spent the first year of his life, it hit me that he was leaving behind his home, his friends, and all he knew for a new life in a new land. And he knew it too. As we turned to leave, he looked back at his companions and his nurses and smiled. Then he grabbed me tightly with one hand and waved good-bye with the other.

I was told that Victor might not bond to us right away and that it was common for new adoptees and their parents to take some time to get used to each other. That didn't turn out to be

Victor and his mother, Pat Locke

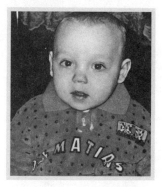

Victor Locke as a baby

the case. Victor and I bonded quickly and deeply, becoming each other's anchors through life's journey. We had both taken that leap of faith into the unknown. And while we've certainly had ups and downs along the way since then, it's been the ride of a lifetime.

My husband and I are no longer together, but we're good friends and still love each other very much. Victor is now an energetic and creative twelve-year-old who drives me absolutely crazy, but he is thriving in school, loves music and movies, and has a terrific group of friends. We laugh and fight and enjoy all kinds of adventures, just as all families do. When he was little, people used to tell me how lucky Victor was that I "saved" him. I would just smile and shake my head, saying that I was the lucky one for having Victor save me. And wherever life takes us, I know that I'll always feel that way.

PATRICIA RYAN LAMPL

Patricia Ryan Lampl is an author and television producer who lives in New York with her husband, Mark, and their daughter, Sophie.

Occasionally, when I sit with the other mommies at nursery school, waiting to pick up my daughter, Sophie, the subject of labor will come up. The moms discuss their labors and deliveries in great detail. "Pat, how long was your labor?" someone invariably asks, forgetting that Sophie is my daughter through adoption. "Six years," I'll answer. "It was long and painful, and like yours, worth every minute."

MARCH/APRIL 1994

I'm getting married to a wonderful man with two children. Since I'm not some ingénue, we throw "the protection" away before the wedding, even though I have a secret fear that I'll be pregnant at the ceremony. Note: If you want to see God laugh, tell Her your plans.

I make a gynecologist appointment and ask, "Am I too old? Is everything working?" "Pat," she replies, "if anyone under thirty comes in my office, I think they have the wrong address. Have fun. If nothing happens in six months, we'll talk."

AUGUST 1994

We're talking.

JANUARY 1995 TO MARCH 1998

I've entered the infertility factory. Everything is calm, efficient, and hygienic, but anxiety, manifested as faux calm, could blow the roof off the waiting room. We're all members of a club that we don't want to belong to. Eye contact is nonexistent. I make a mental note that there is a 30 percent success rate. What I don't account for is the difference between pregnancies and deliveries. After preliminary testing, blood work, sonograms, ultrasounds, and more, Mark and I receive our stash of plastic specimen cups. This is every man's nightmare. He's a knight in shining armor carrying a plastic cup. We are escorted to a block of rooms equipped with magazines and videos. The men "go in" and the women sit on a bench reading. Every woman sits like a statue except for the bouncing foot. Some kick line . . .

One morning I realize that I've read the same paragraph in the *New York Times* for twenty minutes. After a number of months, Mark opts for the home performance with his cup. I vow that when it is all over, I'll host a Tupperware party with one-size cup and one color lid.

Sonograms . . . Ultrasounds . . . Blood work . . . More blood work . . . Miscarriage #1 . . . Progesterone . . . Miscarriage #2 . . . Shots . . . Acupuncture . . . Yoga . . . Shots . . . Miscarriages.

I know if I do yoga I'll be calm and centered. Even though for me, being calm and centered is impossible. Feeling angry, tense, disappointed, hopeful, and exhausted is the norm.

Miscarriage #3: I see another doctor known in the pipeline as having a more "holistic" approach. The office feels nearly warm and fuzzy. There's no sign-in sheet. Real compassion.

Miscarriage #4: There are days when it's hard to get out of bed. I can't go to other people's baby showers. When someone complains about sleep deprivation from a newborn, I could go postal.

Miscarriage #5: I've hit my ceiling. I know this isn't going to happen even though I've followed the rules.

OCTOBER 1998

I try to make peace with not becoming a mother. One day while running errands with my four-year-old neighbor, Robbie, we have the following conversation:

"Mrs. Lampl, how come you don't have a baby?"
"I don't know, Robbie."
"But I want you to have one."
"So do I. But you don't always get what you want."
"How come you don't have one?"
"I guess there's something broken in my stomach."
"I'll fix it."
"I don't think you can."

"Maybe a doctor can."

"We've been to a lot of doctors and they couldn't."

"Maybe God can."

"Rob, maybe God has other plans for me."

"Mrs. Lampl, I don't want you to be lonely."

"I'm not, Rob. I have Mr. Lampl."

"But that's different."

Yes, it is.

My husband returns home and I drop the bombshell. I may not be able to be pregnant, but that doesn't mean I can't be a mother. I want to adopt. We decide to proceed. I don't think I've ever felt so loved in my life.

MARCH 1999

We do extensive research, attend a seminar with Dr. Jane, and sign with an adoption agency. We'll adopt from Russia, and so begins the mountain of paperwork. It's quite startling to go from a process that's medically impersonal to the personally invasive adoption process, which includes letters of reference, medical histories, home study, financial statements, police clearances, blood tests, and fingerprinting. On second thought, maybe more people should do this before they become parents.

JULY 1999

A video arrives via FedEx. I wait until Mark comes home to look at it. After all we've been through together, there's no way I'll watch it without him.

We hit "play." Video hash. She looks up at the camera at us, her parents. We both start crying. There she is, our daughter. We've found each other.

AUGUST TO SEPTEMBER 1999

We complete stacks of immigration paperwork and wait to receive the word that we can travel. Our agency and Dr. Jane hold our hands and guide us throughout the entire process.

Mark's children respond with a love and generosity of spirit for which I'll always love them. We're counting the moments until we get on the plane. I'm out of my skin because my daughter is in the world and I'm not holding her.

SEPTEMBER 30, 1999

JFK airport has never looked so good. We arrive in Moscow and complete more paperwork and then fly to Yekaterinburg.

My legs are like Jell-O when I walk into the building. We're only allowed thirty minutes with her, and I'm sure my heart will break when we have to leave. We're required to visit three times before our court appearance where we'll be declared her parents.

Once our court appearance is complete and her passport is issued, we're done. We burn the phone lines to our families and friends who've been with us every step of the way. Feeding our daughter mashed bananas in a hotel room in Russia, cobbled together tooth and nail, we're a family.

LIZ GRAY

Liz Gray lives with her husband, Ted, on Long Island, New York, with their five children, one of whom was adopted from Guinea-Bissau, West Africa, July 2, 2011.

Our Journey

My Dear Sweet Boy Fabian Nathaniel Gray,

I am sitting on the plane ready to take off for Dakar, Senegal. My cousin Michael is with me. I chose to wait until this time to track our journey to you because I knew I would be so excited and would need to keep myself busy or I would go crazy.

The next ten days will include flying into Guinea-Bissau to Casa Emanuel, the orphanage where you live, and then on to Dakar, Senegal, to get a U.S. visa to bring you home with me to the U.S. Once in the U.S., we will readopt you. Casa Emanuel's lawyer handled all of the legal work in Guinea-Bissau and then we translated everything from Portuguese to English and applied for a U.S. visa to bring you home. We feel so lucky to be on our way to bring you home!

It has been one year since we started this journey, and eight months since you were born, so I will start at the beginning. Your father and I had always talked about adopting a child or children. My mother (your grandmother) and my uncle were adopted, as were two of your cousins. You were always in our hearts and we just needed to find one another. It's funny *because we do not think or feel that way about most things in our lives; we try to not worry and to let things unfold naturally, but the planner in me always comes out. With you, I just had complete faith in something bigger.*

We had initially started to explore the Ivory Coast, but found out there was a residency requirement of at least two years. After a lot of networking, we ended up working with Casa Emanuel in Guinea-Bissau. I told the contact at the orphanage about Dad and me, your brothers, Reilly, Flynn, and Johnny, your sister, Frankie, and our dream of expanding our family through adoption. We were introduced to an American family who had adopted three children from Casa Emanuel. We completed our home study and started putting together all the papers we needed.

Your father and I worked very hard on the paperwork; we needed to get birth certificates, financial records, a copy of our marriage license, and lots more. Never once did we think of giving up. With each document we knew we were getting closer to you!

On November 17, 2010, Maritza, who speaks English and who became my constant contact with you (and who I will always love for bringing us together) wrote us to say you had been born! Her e-mail title was "IT'S A BOY!!" I will never forget it. We did not know when or how you would come to us, but the second I saw that e-mail, I knew you were our son. She told us how your birth uncle taught physics at Casa Emanuel, and his cousin's wife had given birth to you and died a few hours later unexpectedly. Your birth uncle convinced your birth father to bring you to Casa Emanuel, where you would be cared for and fed. It was a very difficult decision for him because he loved you so much. I met your birth father much later in the process, when I saw in person how great his love was for you.

The next eight months seemed endless. Casa Emanuel sent us some photos, and even one video of you, which kept us going. I found the nighttime particularly hard because I thought of you and worried. I wondered if you were sleeping and if someone was there to comfort you when you cried, and I prayed that somehow you knew we were coming soon. In April, we received the documents that legally made you our son in Guinea-Bissau.

Once our I-600 was approved, we contacted the American Embassy in Dakar and set up an appointment. It was time to bring you home!!! Dad arranged all the travel plans for cousin Michael and me. He was very sad to not be coming with me, but prepared everything at home for your arrival. Your brothers and sister and our friends made signs and purchased balloons and eagerly awaited your arrival.

Our first moments together were magical, although you were quiet and maybe a little scared; you reached for me from your crib and in an instant, we were both "home." On the plane ride over, I had a great deal of anxiety about what I would feel when I first held you and how you would feel about me. I had given birth to your brothers and sister and knew the instantaneous love when they were handed to me at birth, but I wanted to be prepared if this experience was different. It was not different for me and although I cannot speak for you, we definitely held each other's gaze and seemed to have a mutual understanding that we had both been waiting for this moment.

III.

The Moment We Met

NGUYEN, NAM VAN A OR B (BEN)

I loved him from the minute I saw his photos. I loved the idea of him for sure. My partner and others who saw the first photos saw his sadness. I did too, but I still adored him completely. I loved him even more deeply when I met him on that very hot day in Hanoi in August 2000. I flew through the doors of the orphanage and almost demanded to know where he was; his name was Nam Van Nguyen and there were two children with this name: one was "A" and the other was "B." Bobo, the facilitator for the adoption agency, located him in his crib. I scooped him up in my arms and held him tightly. He stared blankly with his head turned to one side. I was mesmerized. He was eighteen weeks old.

My partner, Diana, and I took Ben (named by Diana for my brother, Barry), back to the Hanoi Towers hotel. He was wearing a onesie from Sears, most likely donated by an American family who had come through the "feeding center" (as orphanages are called in Vietnam) at Tu Liem for their adoption. We undressed him and changed his diaper, all the while talking and smiling at him, trying to make him happy. In the taxi on the way to the hotel, Diana made him smile. On the videotape I made of him in those early hours, Diana says out loud while talking to him in a high-pitched voice, "He needed to smile."

He worked very hard at everything. That was sad and yet I don't recall feeling sad at the time. I was so crazy for this boy that nothing was going to take that away. My style of parenting was established from the first moment I met Ben. I was aware of his delays and his depression, but I was his mama and I loved him unconditionally. That he didn't smile and that his hands were balled into fists didn't matter to me. That he was in most ways withdrawn and uncomfortable with himself was something I knew could happen with a baby in an orphanage. I look at him now, twelve years later, and he is not depressed or sad; he is an inquisitive and adventurous young man who loves his family, his school, his pet cockatiel, Rico, and his home, and when he goes somewhere, he is eager and adaptive.

He was seated on my lap at a local Hanoi café (frequented by Catherine Deneuve when she filmed *Indochine*); his leg had a tremor and the skin appeared mottled. I repositioned him and these unusual symptoms subsided. I pointed it out to Diana. Even with all my experience treating children from orphanages, I was puzzled. We took him to the clinic on Hai Ba Trung in Hanoi for a checkup. He had some fungus (thrush) in his mouth, and the doctor saw the mottling and the tremor but had no explanation. The doctor also diagnosed Ben's acquired torticollis, a shortening of the neck muscles likely the result of birth trauma and chronic immobility in the crib at the orphanage.

He slept through the night and sucked down his bottles fast. He napped diligently cuddled up on his little blanket across two chairs as we ate lunch and dinner in restaurants in Hanoi and Ho Chi Minh City. Ben was in most ways a very easy baby. He seemed to enjoy our frivolity and eagerness. We enjoyed the day-in and day-out tasks of making him comfortable. After three weeks in Vietnam, we took him home to New York to start our lives as a family.

MARY-LOUISE PARKER

Mary-Louise is an actress who lives in New York with her two children.

My daughter had been left alone in a playpen in an empty room at the orphanage so I could meet her in private, and she was crying. This was a good orphanage, with loving, responsible caregivers, but still, an orphanage is an orphanage, and there are only so many pairs of hands and so many blankets to go around. Being left in an empty room was probably terrifying for her, whereas being crowded and fighting for attention had become what was safe and familiar. Seeing her for the first time was all kinds of overwhelming, but I was fortified by the trust she showed me when I picked her up and she put her head on my shoulder. She seemed relieved. She stopped crying, and I saw the beginnings of this bright little girl who now ropes in almost everyone she meets. I don't know really how else to say it, but she sparkles.

The next day, when one of the nurses at the orphanage came to take my daughter from my arms, she pulled away and latched on to me, much in the same way my son did when he was that age and a stranger held out his or her arms. The caregiver gave a little gasp. I thought at first that maybe she felt wounded, but then she called one of the other nannies over. She gestured for her to watch, and she reenacted trying to take Ash from me. Ash would have none of it. The two nannies laughed and chattered to each other, and I asked an English-speaking nurse what they were saying. "They are happy for her," she said, "They are saying, 'Look at her, she knows already that's mother, she knows it, she won't go to us.'" She was sure she knew that I was her mother and that my son was her brother.

The two of them looked at each other with nothing less than agreement when my son told her that we were now a three family; before we were the two family, and now we were the three family. "We're the three Parker family, Ash. Pick her up, Mommy, hug her!" he practically shouted while marching around the room. "So you're my sister, I'm your brother, we're gonna take a big plane and it bumps when it goes down, but don't worry, you won't have to wear that little yellow thing for breathing, it won't come down. The plane will be safe and then we'll go home. It's gonna be great."

They knew everything before I truly processed it; they knew who they were to each other, and nothing . . . nothing on earth makes me happier than when they walk down the street holding hands, or defend each other, or unite together against someone. Even when that someone is me, I'm still silently cheering.

SUSAN KASSLER-TAUB

*Susan Kassler-Taub is a social worker in Princeton, New Jersey.
She and her husband, Ken, have three children, the youngest of
whom was adopted from Borovichi, Russia.*

IT WAS THE EYES

FAITH

*When you walk to the edge of all the light you have
and take that first step into the darkness of the unknown,
you must believe that one of two things will happen:*

*There will be something solid for you to stand upon,
or, you will be taught how to fly*

—PATRICK OVERTON

On July 2, 2012, I copied these words onto the first page of my
notebook just before we left for Russia, not fully knowing then
how relevant they would prove to be over the next six days.

As I look back fourteen years later, the shape of the memories
is different now than in the years soon after. In the beginning,
each detail stayed sharp; now I have a series of receding photos in
my memory, interspersed with certain very clear images, as though
in three dimensions, popping out on my visual screen.

Some memories from the very beginning:

It was the eyes.

A few days before, I was sitting at my desk, the phone rang, and I heard the social worker telling me about a baby girl, born in September, who was waiting in Borovichi, Russia. I quickly did the calculations—a four-month-old baby girl. My mind was reeling—did she really just say born in September? As I listened, I wrote copious notes, knowing I was not processing the words I was hearing.

It was in September that we had decided we were ready to move forward with adoption. Sitting in synagogue, reading the familiar liturgy of the High Holy Days, there it was: "On Rosh Hashanah it is *written*, and on Yom Kippur it is *decided*." The word jumped off the page. I'd read this liturgy so many times, but the word in front of me had changed. Past versions of this prayer had always read "sealed"; here, in this new prayer book, the choice was "decided." I knew it was time.

A photo finally arrived a few days later. I opened the envelope, and there she was—it was the eyes, they sparkled right through the simple photo. A tiny baby, in a plain smock, held aloft by strong hands, staring right at the camera, with those eyes. It was decided.

The next days were a whirlwind of preparation; preparing our children who would wait at home for their new sister, gathering everything we would need for our new daughter, and assembling the medical supplies we would bring to the orphanage. The call came to ask if we could leave in just a few days—of course we could. Then another call came the next day to say no, we had to wait two more weeks for the family traveling to Borovichi to be ready. We waited.

Finally we were on the flight, prepared to spend our first night in Moscow and take the train to Borovichi the next morning. We learned quickly in Russia that our job was to go with the flow, trust the coordinator, and ask as few questions as possible. The lessons began immediately. We weren't spending the night in Moscow after all, and there would be no train ride. We were leaving immediately, by van, driving through the day and evening to Borovichi. The vehicle was an old cargo van, the seats appeared to be from other cars and were barely bolted down. There was so little heat in the van that I was very glad to be wearing warm long johns as I watched the windshield ice over. As we drove the many hours, we saw Russians walking along the snow-covered roads and understood the poverty of the countryside. The kindness of our coordinator, translator, and driver was immediately evident—we were in their hands and had to have faith in them.

As we arrived in Borovichi, I tentatively asked if we would see our daughter that night. "Unlikely," said our coordinator, Vera; instead we would have dinner in a restaurant, go to the hotel, and see her in the morning. The restaurant was traditional, and we were put at a table upstairs, hidden from the locals. Vera left for a few minutes, and when she returned, we were told we were going to the orphanage immediately. Next lesson: we would be given information only just before we needed to know, and over the five days that followed, we learned to relinquish all the obsessive planning that had gotten us this far.

The brightest memory, the one that will never fade: back in the van, driving to the orphanage. It is nearly midnight and I don't know when we last slept. The streets of Borovichi are empty. A light snow is falling as we pull into the orphanage compound. Dark brick buildings covered in snow. We walk up the brightly lit front steps; the building is silent; I am certain I am holding my breath. We are brought into an anteroom, which is decorated for the children, colorful and warm. We wait the longest few minutes, and a nurse appears holding a tiny bundle tightly wrapped in a pink blanket. The nurse places our daughter in my arms, just woken from sleep; she stares at us with those twinkling eyes, and smiles.

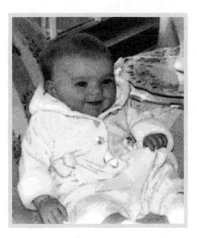

Charlotte Kassler-Taub, who was adopted from Borovichi, Russia, lives with her family in New Jersey.

LIA BRADLEY

Lia Bradley was born in Anhui Province, China, in 1997, and lives in New York City with her parents, younger sister, Maya, and dog, Scooter. Now in high school, Lia enjoys gymnastics, singing, and photography. This memoir about adopting her sister was a middle school English project. Lia obsesses over heartthrob Justin Bieber and UK bands One Direction and The Wanted.

It's early in the morning. I'm still trying to get the sleep out of my eyes, looking at a beautiful sunrise framed by white and pink clouds. I've been on this plane for twenty-four endless hours. Finally we've landed. My ears are plugged and I want to get this funny feeling out of my stomach. I'm nervous and excited, and maybe hungry.

It's December 2003, I'm six years old, and I'm in China. I'm here with my mommy and daddy. Just the three of us—that's our family. But things are about to change. We've come here to get my baby sister.

Ever since I can remember, I've always wanted a baby sister. In my mind, I had a picture of me, pushing a stroller down the sidewalk. Inside the stroller is a little baby who looks up at me with a loving heart. I bend over and fix her blanket and touch her cheek. She holds my finger with her whole hand.

I used to ask my mom, just about every day, "Mom, can I have a sister?" Maybe I was lonely. I wanted to bond with someone. The answer was always, "Honey, I'm sorry, we just can't do it."

But one day, my mom said yes. She told me there's an orphan in China. She's one year old, and she needs a family.

So here we are.

We go to a city called Wuhan, because that's where my sister is. We get on a bus and go to the government office. It's so cold inside the building that you can see your breath! My parents are signing papers, and more papers. There are some other adults there, also signing papers. I go to the room next door and play with some other kids while we wait. Then I go back and wait some more with my mom and dad. We sit in the little room, on hard brown benches, waiting, waiting. The room smells so bad, like chemicals, and it's very cold. Finally I hear the sound of crying babies. The door opens and I see babies, about eight of them, being carried in, crying and kicking. Someone calls out "Bradley!" My mom puts out her arms and someone hands her a baby. It's my sister! My mom starts crying. But I'm not crying. I'm so excited. This is my sister. My sister!

I ask mom if I can hold her. When she gives the baby to me, I know that I have the cutest sister ever. She's the littlest thing on earth. I didn't know she would be so little. I hold her very carefully. She looks very scared. I touch her cheek, just like in my dream. I touch her tears. She doesn't cry that much, though. She just makes a sad face and sniffs. Her cheeks are very smooth and rosy. Maybe she's hot. She's wearing three pairs of pants, two shirts, a coat, a hat, and red plastic boots that are way too big.

Wait a minute, something seems really wrong. Her head is totally flat in back. I freak out. "Mom! What's the matter with her head?" My mom says, "It's okay, Lia, I think she was always lying in her crib."

The paperwork's finally finished. We leave the building and get back on the bus. But now there are four of us. My mom is holding my sister. I take a toy out of my bag—it's a set of stacking cups. I hand my sister the purple cup. She loves it. She starts to laugh. When we get back to the hotel, she falls right asleep. Actually, we all fall asleep. We're jet-lagged and worn out and too excited.

The next few days, we're all getting to know each other. My sister likes scrambled eggs and noodles, just like me. Her first dinner is beef and rice. And she says her first English word—"that's." She is so, so cute.

Before my sister can come to the United States, she has to get a visa. So we all go to the city of Guangzhou. Mom and Dad fill out more papers. Then we take my sister to see a doctor. Before someone can go live in America, they have to show that they're healthy.

There's a young Chinese doctor in the hospital room. He looks carefully at Maya, and then listens to her heart with his stethoscope. Then he frowns and shakes his head. "I'm sorry," he tells us, "but this baby has a heart murmur. She may have something wrong with her heart. She's not allowed to leave China." My mom's crying like crazy. I don't understand what's going on, but I know it's bad. The doctor calls some other doctors in, and they're all talking in Chinese. The doctor tells us that this baby might not be healthy. Mom does not let go of my sister. She says, "This is my baby! She is part of our family. We will take care of her." The doctors talk for a long time and finally they agree to sign the papers. (We soon learned when we got home that Maya was absolutely healthy.)

After all that anxiousness with the doctors, I go back to the hotel. I relax, watch TV, and try to teach my sister how to walk and talk. We stay in China for a few more days. Then we get on another plane, and boy, oh boy, what a flight! All I can hear is my sister crying—nothing else—for twenty-four hours.

Though it seems endless, the flight comes to an end at last. We go home and fall right asleep without even taking our clothes off. But before I fall asleep, I say to myself: "I can't believe my dream came true. I finally have a baby sister."

Ruth Mullen and her two daughters, Lia Bradley and Maya Bradley

I am going to China soon with my mom and dad to get my baby sister and her name is maya she is going to live in New york with us and I am so excited and I can't wait!.

ZAYNA MAHBUB

Zayna Aisha Mahbub (age 8) describes meeting her sister Anya for the first time.

After school, I went to the hospital to see my baby sister. She had lots of hair! Most babies don't have hair, but my sister's head had tons of hair, plugged to it. She had dark beautiful eyes. Her hands were even smaller than Albus (class pet). Her feet moved around like CRAZY! I felt confused. I said to myself "What is that monkey doing close to my mom?" Then after a while I knew what I always wanted in my whole life, my very own, little, tiny baby sister. It was one of the most special moments of my life.

ZAYNA AISHA MAHBUB

ANN SILVERBERG

Ann Silverberg is an editor at Newsday *and lives in Garden City, New York, with her husband, Terry Kelleher, and daughter, Jia Kelleher, who studies art at Mount Holyoke College.*

FRIDAY, JULY 8, 1994

It was a frustrating week trying to wring the information about our referral from our Manhattan adoption agency. We learned that our referral had arrived on Tuesday, but our phone call to the agency was not returned that day. Our social worker called on Wednesday but was reluctant to tell us much over the phone. We made an appointment to meet her at her office at ten-thirty a.m. Thursday.

A phone call at seven a.m. Thursday interrupted a night in which sleep did not come easily anyway. It was our social worker saying she was laid low by digestive problems and would be unable to keep our appointment. I politely begged if it would be possible for someone else to share the referral information with us. I watched the O. J. Simpson hearings on TV with half an eye, anxiously awaiting a call from the agency. I finally got through to the international adoption director in the afternoon. She was in a great hurry to get off the phone. I did find out the baby was born on November 25, 1993 (Thanksgiving!), and she was in an Anhui Province orphanage in Anqing, about one hundred miles south of

Hefei, China. The agency promised to meet with me on Friday at twelve-thirty p.m.

Our social worker was feeling better and conducted our meeting in one of the many offices disguised as living rooms. She presented me with a colorful picture of Jia-Jia, a bright-eyed cutie wrapped in a patterned comforter. Jia-Jia's right arm obscured her mouth and chin. She appears to have long fingers and a good grip. A red spot on her forehead which was applied with something like lipstick matched the red background. The health form from the Anhui children's institute indicated that as of March 14, 1994, Jia-Jia had not had any serious disease but had diaper rash and "needed nutriment."

We were promised that we would be informed of any new information about our departure date. It was 94 degrees outside—a record high. As I left the agency with Jia-Jia's picture safely in my purse, it was raining. I got to the number 6 subway stop at 96th and Lexington well sprinkled. I stood in front of a fan in the steamy subway station and got blow-dried waiting for the train to come. There was a delay at 51st Street, where I was to switch to the E train to get back to Penn Station. The muffled announcement indicated the next train would be coming in five minutes. People were lined up three deep and it was miserably hot. A street musician started strumming her guitar and singing a gospel-type song about counting your blessings. I started counting and Jia-Jia was at the top of my list.

When I got home, I looked up "Jia" in our *Chinese in 10 Minutes a Day* book and found it meant "home." My husband, Terry, checked the Pinyin dictionary at work and found that "Jia" means dozens of things, among them "good," "fine," "beautiful," "gal," and "family." The name Jia has great appeal.

THURSDAY, JULY 12, 1994

I spent an hour and a half with Dr. Jane Aronson in her Mineola office getting advice on the care and feeding of the baby. I left with suggestions to bring a mirrored toy, a tape player and Raffi music, and baby applesauce; a prescription for vitamins, diaper rash ointment, Maltsupex for constipation, and medicine for ear infections were provided in this pre-travel session. When I offered to pay for the visit, Dr. Aronson said, "No, I should pay you."

TUESDAY, JULY 19, 1994

I shared the baby's picture with *Newsday* colleague Jeff Sommer, a former Beijing correspondent and now the foreign editor. He determined that "Jia" meant "good, excellent, admirable." I asked him to help me learn a phrase in Mandarin to say when the baby is presented to us in Hefei. Here it is in pidgin Pinyin:

Hsieh hsieh neimen dui haidzi dwoma how. ("Thank you for being so good to the child.")

THURSDAY, JULY 28, 1994 (JIA DAY!)

The flight from Beijing to Hefei took an hour and a half, and we landed about noon, forgoing the China Air sweet snacks and the boxed lychee juice. It was well over 90 degrees when we landed. Our group of three couples and four single women on the cusp of parenthood crowded our luggage into some vans and ourselves into others for the ride to the Anhui Hotel. Terry and I checked into room 1402 with its empty purple crib and then went down to lunch in the hotel dining room. We bypassed menu offerings of dove and bullfrog, opting for the more familiar boiled dumplings, fried rice, and lemon chicken.

Xiong Yan, the agency's tireless facilitator in China, had said that she would start bringing the babies around to our rooms at three p.m. As the hour approached, we nervously paced the hall. Just about three p.m., we saw the orphanage staff arrive in Xiong Yan's room with a parade of babies. We spotted one particularly adorable girl in an elaborate yellow dress and a white hat with a ruffled visor. Xiong Yan then walked down the hall with three men and two women, whom she identified as coming from Anqing. It was Jia-Jia, which they pronounced "Jah-Jah." She was absolutely beautiful and so sweet. We oohed and aahed over her in the hallway and then invited the Anqing delegation into our room. An elderly nurse, obviously attached to the baby, proudly carried her. Jia-Jia seemed interested in her new teddy bear rattle and her squeaking caterpillar toy. She admired herself in the hand mirror that Dr. Aronson had suggested. In our atonal Chinese, Terry and I together said, *"Hsieh hsieh neimen dui haidzi dwoma how,"* our practiced but sincere thank you.

At four p.m., all seven families and the orphanage representatives were instructed to meet in a second-floor conference room for a process called "registration." The paperwork required us to pledge our perpetual support for Jia's well-being. It also required red-inked thumbprints from us and a footprint from Jia. That required removing one of her quilted shoes.

It was clear that Jia was well loved by the orphanage representatives, particularly the nurse who gave her special care; I saw the nurse tear up as the Anqing delegation bade us a long good-bye.

We took Jia back upstairs, and for the first time, she was fussy. We tried all the tricks up our short sleeves, but she was not easily consoled. Her tears lingered on her cheeks. We couldn't get her to take a bottle or spoon-fed rice cereal, but how she loved her first Cheerios! Eventually she was lulled to sleep by the lullabies on the Raffi tape. At this writing, I don't know if she's down for the night or merely napping.

DIANA LEO

Diana has three children, a twenty-four-year-old daughter and two sons ages fourteen and twelve. All her children were adopted. She lives with her partner and sons in New Jersey. Another piece by Diana appears on page 154.

There are two stories, anecdotes really, that I'd like to share about the domestic adoption of my oldest child. I was forty-one when I began the process, which was through a private adoption lawyer, and just a month shy of my forty-second birthday when I flew to Arizona to pick up my newly born daughter.

While I was waiting for her birth, I read every book written (it seemed) on babies, the first year of life, the superb mother, the great mother, the good enough mother, and the not any good mother. You can imagine which I was aiming for.

My partner (at the time) and I flew out to Arizona the day before we were due to receive the baby and go to court for custody. I went to the lawyer's office to await her return with the baby and her birth mother from their court date at which the birth mother was ceding maternal rights. I was sure that something could still go awry and was in a state of suspended emotions.

When they walked into the room, the baby, only five days old, was completely swaddled, with mitts on her hands and an infant cap on her head. The only thing I could see were two closed eyes, a tiny nose, and a rosebud mouth.

When I left that office, I was carrying my daughter in my arms, terrified that I would trip on the pavement and drop her on her head, mainly because my eyes were so filled with tears. I made it up to the hotel room, where my partner was anxiously awaiting me—no, us. Gently, carefully, worshipfully, we placed the sleeping infant in the middle of our bed, and then silently and slowly, we unwrapped her.

Don't ask me what I was expecting, but when I saw her perfect beautiful body, my first thought was a terrified "It's a baby—oh my God, what do I do now?"

What I did was to almost starve her to death. We had been given a starter package of formula, diapers, wipes, etc. As the baby started to stir and smack her lips, we continued to stare at her. Gradually, the stirring became flailing and the smacking became a shrieking cry of hunger. "A bottle!" I screamed. "She's hungry—she needs a bottle." I lunged for the formula but could not unscrew the lid. The screams grew louder. My partner grabbed it from me and held the lid under burning hot water. The screams grew louder still. I took the bottle, prepared to smash it against the side of the sink, when with one final twist, the cap flew off, the nipple went on, and we stuck it in the baby's mouth.

I burst into tears. "I can't do this," I sobbed. "I'm not ready."

That was twenty-four years and three children ago.

JOSHUA HARRISON AND
LAURIE STRICKS

Joshua produces media and interactive programming and his wife, Laurie Stricks, is a clinical psychologist. They live in New York City with their daughter, Ana Sofia, who was adopted from Guatemala.

ANA SOFIA HARRISON: THE DAY WE MET

We adopted Ana Sofia from Guatemala in 2003. It was a complicated time for international adoptions from Guatemala. The country was under a lot of pressure to become Hague Convention compliant, which would require complete reorganization of their system for managing international adoptions. The political situation in the country was tense, and rumors of ending international adoption abounded. As a result, we spent months in and out of political limbo while waiting to meet our daughter. At one point, after we got our assignment and had seen our first photos of our daughter, we heard that the entire system was shutting down. We were terrified of losing her to politics and had visions of moving to Guatemala and staying there for however long it would take to work it out.

Fortunately, we managed to work through all the initial paperwork, the medical exams, the multiple attestations and court-mandated appearances, and were able to make our first visit to meet Ana Sofia, then four months old. That visit was a wonder and a blur. No matter how much we prepared, how much we read or researched or compared notes with family and friends who already had kids, we still felt nervous about taking on the awesome responsibility for a new life.

At the very least, we thought we would have a gradual introduction to our child. We would arrive in the capital, find our hotel, and have an evening to gain our bearings. We would meet our daughter and her foster mother for a brief visit the next day, then we would spend a little more time the following day, all under the benevolent and watchful gaze of our agency. It didn't quite work out that way.

We called Lucy, the foster mother, the day we arrived to make an appointment for an initial visit. Twenty minutes later, a white Ford Explorer drives up to the front of the hotel and a woman gets out holding an infant swaddled in a blue and white blanket. The woman has a smile as large as a harvest moon, and she walks over to me and my wife and hands me a bundle containing four-month-old Ana Sofia. She then turns to Laurie, my wife, and they wrap their arms around each other. They are hugging and crying tears of joy. I can barely keep myself from joining them. I give Ana Sofia to Laurie, who holds this tiny bundle with an amazingly wise and serene face, and the tears just keep streaming down her face even as she lights up the entire front hallway of the hotel with her smile.

Laurie and I are hugging each other and holding Ana Sofia, who is calmly taking in what's happening around her. We're overflowing with feelings. She's the most beautiful thing in the world; we were exhausted, adoption weary, nervous, indescribably complete, and instantly in love.

Then Lucy hands us a bag with diapers, baby bottles, a few clothes, and some formula. She talks to us about the baby's routine: how much she eats, when she sleeps, what she likes. She then gives us each another hug and says to call her with any questions. Slightly stunned, but deliriously happy, we go up to our room in the hotel and begin our lives together as a family.

TERRY HAAS

Terry Haas is married to Mary Ann Betsch, the love of his life, and they live in New York with their one-year-old son, Jote, whom they adopted from Ethiopia in 2012.

Monday, March 5th, 2012 (5:56 p.m.)

Good afternoon!

We received word from the staff in Ethiopia that your case has been assigned a court date of March 15, 2012!

We are thrilled you will be traveling to Ethiopia. It is truly an exciting time! Please arrange your air travel so that you arrive in Addis Ababa anytime on Monday, March 12, or the morning of Tuesday, March 13, 2012; and depart Addis Ababa March 16, 2012.

This is the e-mail we received ten days before our court date to adopt our son from Ethiopia. We needed to leave the United States in six days! The week prior to meeting him was filled with logistics, including tying up loose ends at work, arranging flights, and managing the contractors at our home. We didn't have time to imagine how wonderfully our lives would change in just ten short days.

We landed in Addis Ababa, Ethiopia, and arrived at the guesthouse at eleven-thirty p.m. on the following Monday. We were told that the morning pickup for the trip to the orphanage was set for six-thirty a.m. We had no time to process the excitement and we tossed and turned all night. The drive was three hours, and we spent most of that time looking at the countryside and imagining that his birth family was in one of the villages we passed. After three hours of anticipation, we pulled up to the orphanage. Our nerves were really kicking in now.

We entered the main room, where he was sharing a crib with another baby. We finally were face-to-face with our son. He looked at us with bewildered eyes, yet he seemed to know we were his mom and dad. He had the most wonderful smile and the cutest little birthmark on his forehead. We brought clothes and toys for the orphanage, and our social worker quickly found an outfit for him and we started opening toys.

Like any eight-month-old, he was more interested in the cardboard boxes than the toys themselves. We sat on the ground and banged on some boxes and rolled some balls, but he kept wanting to be hugged and held by his mom. Between hugs, he showed us what he could do. He was crawling around so fast we knew we had an active boy with an unquenchable curiosity. He explored everything with so much interest, especially the iPhones we were using to take pictures and videos. At one point he crawled to a chair, looked at it, and used it to stand himself up, at just eight months old! We only had an hour and a half with him during our first visit, but I think the last twenty minutes proved we were meant to be a family. We went outside to get a little sun, and he started snuggling with Mom and a slipped his right thumb in his mouth (we now know this is his signal for a nap). Mom propped him on her knee, and as she rubbed his back, his eyes got heavy and he drifted off to sleep. It might sound a little weird, but some of the best time of our first meeting was while he was asleep. How many adoptive parents get to tuck their children in and kiss them good night the first time they meet?

On the way home, we talked about our feelings about leaving

him. It was sad and easy at the same time. He was so loved at his orphanage in his first eight months that we knew there was no better place for him to wait until we came to take him home to the United States.

We had an assortment of normal emotions during our visit, but the reality never hit until our court date. At the end of our hearing, we had to confirm our desire to adopt him because the decree would be final. We could hardly speak and whatever we said came out like gibberish in a flood of tears of joy. We just nodded, hoping the judge understood our happiness.

It was three days from our first meeting to our court date, and they were the most amazing three days of our lives.

ELENI COFFINAS

*Eleni Coffinas is a partner at a Manhattan law firm. She resides
in Brooklyn with her husband, Michael DiRaimondo, and her
daughter, Nicole (almost six), who was adopted from China when
she was fourteen months old. Michael, who has two grown sons
ages twenty-nine and thirty, fell in love with Nicole at first sight in
China and is now in the process of finalizing his adoption of her.*

THE WAIT AND AGAIN

The Moment finally arrived on October 8, 2007. The long wait
that had begun three years earlier when I filled out an application
was about to end. The eight-thousand-mile, twenty-hour plane trip
brought me to a gray building with an institutional feel in Guangzhou, China, where my daughter was waiting. She too had endured a long wait and a long journey. I may never know exactly
where her journey began, but her report indicates that at around
eight days of life she was left at an outdoor marketplace and then
found and placed in an orphanage, where she lived and waited for
fourteen months. On that day in October, after a five-hour car ride
from the orphanage, she too had arrived at this somewhat mysterious waiting place.

The wait had the feel of "forever." The seasons changed and
returned. Life continued while it stood still. I was told by an angel
here on earth in Utah, named Stefani, the China program coordi-

nator at my adoption agency, that I did a great job of waiting. I think this is because as the months became years, I inwardly and deeply understood that the years would dissolve into hours and for just one moment time would stand still and the waiting would stop. I replayed that Moment over and over and over again in my head. I lived it and breathed it. In many ways I became it. I watched it in my mind and convinced myself that through the intense fear of uncertainty and distance yet remaining in time, the Moment was on its way.

The wait became too long to allow my father to meet his seventh grandchild. She will know how much he loved her while he was waiting. She already knows that he gave her the gift of a beautiful name and blessed her with her very own angel. The good of the wait was that the man who would become her father showed up just in time. He too loved her before he met her and this made the last part of the journey serene, sweet, and complete. He made it his mission to forever capture that very first Moment when my daughter would be placed in my arms and make me a mother. The photograph is proudly in my four-and-a-half-year-old daughter's princess room. She looks at it and she loves it. She understands that Moment and recently drew her own interpretation of it.

That first Moment played out for real, the way I dreamed it would. I had an overwhelming feeling of calm. And so did she. I watched as she was being carried by a woman whose face and language were familiar to her. As they approached, my arms stretched out waiting, ready to receive. She was so courageous, so cute, and so calm. I believe from deep within my core that the instant she entered my arms, she understood that she was home.

As I gently received her and placed her next to my heart, I whispered in her ear that I would hold her forever. And now, almost four years later, she will often announce, "Mom, today is holding day," and every time she does, I still hold her, and every time, I still think about that first promise.

She arrived without tears but also without a smile. I found myself waiting yet again. And the minutes became hours and the hours became days. No smile. I remember on day three when I was even funnier than usual, she looked up at me and for less than a second started to smile, then quickly looked away with that almost but not quite smile following her gaze, then fading away. She wanted to smile but intentionally held back. In that moment, I understood that she had to make sure that this was for real. She had to be cautious and that caution was probably one of the early instincts she learned to survive.

But then, finally, it happened on day five. We were sitting together in the same chair in a restaurant in the White Swan Hotel, where she began a never-ending love affair with mozzarella

Michael DiRaimondo, Nicole Coffinas, and Eleni Coffinas

cheese. She just smiled. It was the most beautiful smile I had ever seen. We all smiled and then laughed for hours and days and now years. That long wait truly ended, especially for her, with the sweet surrender of that first smile. She was at ease and at peace. It took her fourteen months and me forty-six years to find our "forever family."

MARCIA FAVALE

Marcia has her own advisory business and lives in New York with her family.

They say that it happens in a blink of an eye. Your life can change in an instant. This is a story about such an instant when we were given a small, settled, and determined baby.

Our journey to adopt our precious daughter was complete and definite. Many people write or tell stories of how they underwent a heart-wrenching experience when their children were presented to them. They suffered intense anxiety, worrying what it would be like when their child was finally in their arms. "What if I don't bond?" "What if there's no connection?" This was not our story.

This story is complete in its simplicity. We don't choose—they do. This sense of relinquishing was the first step in the story of our family. Adults fancy themselves in control, and some even consider themselves to be all-knowing. How misguided we are.

Staring at a room full of children on a bleak, cold Kazakh afternoon, waiting to be given my child, the thought of holding her in my arms, I had overwhelming feelings that were a mixture of love, concern, anxiety, and an emotional sense of unknowing.

But then, something pulled my eyes to a corner of the room. There she was, in the arms of a caretaker, looking determined and settled. We locked eyes. In that instant, as if she always knew and had simply been waiting for us, she claimed me, she claimed us, and she claimed her family.

I can't remember much else from that afternoon other than the feeling of holding my baby girl in my arms. There were also lots of smiles. I recall the ease with which she nestled in my arms and with which she trusted. It was as it should be and there was stillness in the universe. All was right in the world. Our purpose was finally clear. I smiled, acknowledging how I was misguided until that moment. We often worry about the silliest things.

In this moment, all else blurred and faded. All the annoyances of the world were of less importance, of no consequence, or simply nonexistent. I do recall whispering in her ear, as if guided or summoned by another me, saying, "I have been looking for you all my life."

Then, in another instant, there we were, a complete family. Standing outside the baby house, we were finally ready to take Alexandra home, to her home, where she always belonged. As we waited outside, saying the emotional good-byes to the wonderful people who took care of our daughter, Alexandra's eyes canvassed the outdoors and settled on her family. I believed she smiled with her eyes. Then she placed her arms around my neck and held tightly. I certainly smiled.

Stillness changed into anxiety as the car pulled away. I had anxiety about bringing Alexandra into a world we can't control and where we can't fully protect her, though we knew we'd give our lives to do so. We can only provide her with the moral, mental, emotional, and physical strength to arm herself. Then in that instant, a most marvelous moment, we knew, as a family, that Alexandra was the most precious thing in our lives.

Thank you, my daughter, for choosing us. In that instant you changed our lives.

CONNIE BRITTON

Connie Britton is an actress who splits her time between Los Angeles, New York, and occasionally Africa. In 2011, she adopted a nine-month-old boy from Ethiopia named Yoby.

In 2004, I took my first trip to Ethiopia. I went to film documentary footage of a young orphan girl who had become pregnant and given birth to a baby who was possibly going to be adopted by a woman in the United States. I had developed an interest in the orphans of Ethiopia, inspired by a friend who was very involved with orphanages in and around Addis Ababa, and who was, in fact, the financial caretaker of the orphan girl we were filming as well as her siblings.

I remember that before I set off on my journey, friends said to me, "Oh, you're going to come back with a baby." How little they or I, for that matter, knew about the process of adoption.

At that time, my mother was suffering from stage 4 breast cancer. She died at the age of sixty-two, shortly after my return from Ethiopia. My father was also suffering from an unusual blood disease called myelodysplastic anemia. He died three years after my mom, almost to the day, at age sixty-five.

After my father's death, I had my own experience of being an orphan. While I never want to make a direct comparison to the millions of children around the world orphaned at birth or at a young age, living in extreme conditions and poverty, there's a sense of groundlessness, and of enormous loss, which I imagine is universal after your parents die.

I was single and had no children, and had for many years thought, "Someday, I'd like to adopt." Suddenly it occurred to me, "What am I waiting for?"

I began to look into adopting from Ethiopia. I did a little research and found an agency with a good reputation. I started the process and was immediately overwhelmed with the most paperwork I had ever encountered for any application in my entire life. I found the process to be painstaking, intrusive, bureaucratic, impersonal, and, of course, time-consuming. Since I was on location, and trying to compile everything in my spare moments while working full-time, it took me almost a year to complete everything.

Once the final government clearance for which I'd applied was received by the adoption agency, the big day arrived. I was officially put on the waiting list for a child. I had applied to adopt a boy or girl under the age of twelve months. At the time, the wait for a referral for a child that age was estimated to be twelve to eighteen months.

During the time that I was on that waiting list, a lot changed in the Ethiopian adoption process, much of which I didn't understand. I will never forget the day that I got a memo from my agency that there was some concern that the Ethiopian government might eliminate adoption by single women. This came almost a year into my being on the waiting list. I was devastated that, with almost two years already invested, I might not be permitted to adopt a child. The feeling of powerlessness was overwhelming.

After my first year of waiting, other changes took place in Ethiopia that lengthened the estimated waiting time for an infant adoption. It was now eighteen to twenty-four months. I'll admit, the wait was becoming excruciating. I was starting to lose hope and actually began to look into domestic adoption.

Then on June 21, 2011, just a couple weeks shy of my two-year marker on the waiting list, I got a call from the social worker at my agency. She asked how the weather was in L.A., and said that she hoped she wasn't calling too early because of the time difference. Then she said she had a possible referral for me. In that moment, my life changed forever. I eagerly listened as she explained the referral procedure, and then I waited the few minutes it took for her to e-mail me the official referral. Once I got it, I looked briefly at the forms and paperwork that accompanied it but quickly scrolled down, hoping for a picture.

And there he was, Eyob. I learned that Eyob is the Amharic version of the biblical name Job, whom many in Africa consider to be the hero of the Bible because he is tested and never loses his faith in God. This was my son. And I was in love. His big dark eyes were looking up at me, present, smiling, waiting. It's the strangest thing, but from that moment on, we were connected.

There is more waiting in store because his trip home is reliant on the Ethiopian government's process, which now requires two trips to Ethiopia for prospective parents to ensure their commitment to the child, legal and otherwise. And so I wait until the time that they say I can come and get my son. But now we are waiting together. And that in itself is something.

AN UPDATE

Eyob is a spectacular, heartful, soulful, cheerful, and ever curious boy who is at the moment very much enjoying his polar bear outfit for Halloween, which, by the way, was the day one year ago that we went to the U.S. Embassy together in Ethiopia, and he officially became my son.

KATHLEEN (CASEY) SANTYE

Erin Comollo is a first-grade teacher at Far Brook School and lives in New Brunswick, New Jersey, with her husband and two adopted cats. She and her brother were adopted from South Korea, and her sister was adopted in New Jersey.

In 2009, my family experienced the devastating loss of my mom to ALS. Shortly after her passing, my dad shared these letters with us. For the first time, we experienced our adoptions through our mother's eyes and her heart. This is a dedication to my mom and every other parent through adoption for their strength, generosity, and most of all, love.

Erin, Tim and Lauren:

Not flesh of my flesh,
Nor bone of my bone,
But still miraculously my own.
Never forget for a single minute
You didn't grow under my heart, but in it.

Love, Mom

Erin,

Into my arms at last. You came to us after such a long wait to be parents. I was just believing that it would never happen. You finally arrived and you made me a Mom! Daddy and I

were so excited! And so clueless. Nobody knows what it en-
tails to be a parent—no instruction manual, as they say. But
we sure did enjoy you. You were a delight and had a zeal for
life even then, as you do now.

Tim, whom I love to call Timmy,

You came next and I never dreamed we would be blessed
with two children. My dad was dying when we started the
adoption process for you. I was so sad about the thought of
losing him, but the thoughts of you made me look toward
the future and have hope. Our wait for your arrival seemed
like an eternity and I worried as you got older and older in
Korea. I longed to hold you in my arms, I longed to be your
mom. Finally you arrived and you were not too happy to be in
your new surroundings. You never slept in your cute little crib.
We put a mattress on the floor in your room and you and I
slept there, together, every night. You would cling to me until
you finally fell asleep. When you woke up, you would panic
until you reached out and found me at your side. It took time
for you to realize that I would always be there for you.

Lauren,

Your arrival was probably the most amazing of all. We
were busy with two kids and didn't have time to go through all
the paperwork, etc., of adopting another child. In 1990,
10:00 at night, we received a call from the social worker who
had placed Timmy with us. She told us about a little girl who
had been born whose mother wanted her placed with a cer-
tain type of family—a family with other adopted children and
who also lived in the country. She asked if we were interested.

I almost jumped through the phone. Of course we said yes, and she said okay we would be considered and she would let us know what the committee decided! What committee? I had already given you my heart when we said "Yes!" We had to wait a few long days to finally get the answer we had longed for. When you arrived we knew you absolutely were meant to be in OUR family. There has never been any doubt, my dear Lauren, that you belong with us. You made us a family of five.

At Erin's wedding (left to right): Chip Santye, Kathleen (Casey) Santye (seated), Lauren Santye, Erin Comollo, Tim Santye

IV.

Early Challenges

Before we met Ben, there was a hitch in our adoption plans, something that explains part of the eagerness with which I ran into the orphanage that day when we were finally able to travel to Vietnam to bring him home. In July of 2000, five weeks before we were scheduled to travel, an article about international adoption, "The Orphan Ranger," written by Melissa Fay Greene (who graciously contributed the essay "The Science of Happiness" in this book), appeared in *The New Yorker*. I knew the gist of what Melissa would write, based on her many interviews with me over the course of the prior year. Wishing not to appear academic, scientific, and one-dimensional, I had phoned her one day to say that I wanted to be open about my sexuality in the article. I was tired of being a doctor without a real life. With impending parenthood,

I wanted to be as open and honest with readers of the magazine as I planned to be with my child.

I received a call from the social worker from my adoption agency in late July. My dossier to Vietnam was being held in D.C. by the Vietnamese consul. They were questioning something in the application. The social worker was evasive. She then got to the point of her call. "You know that article in *The New Yorker*? Well, it might have been better if you had talked to us beforehand." I could hear the disapproval in her voice. In this moment, I had the terrible realization that something bad could happen in our adoption process and that we might not get Ben. I heard the social worker say, "We will respond to the inquiry about your dossier and get back to you." She said that they needed a character letter or something like that. I never found out who they contacted or what this person ultimately said or wrote on my behalf, but about ten days later I was cleared and we set off in August to get our son.

On our way home, at the U.S. consulate in Saigon, the last stop in the long process to finalize the adoption, I carried Ben to the Plexiglas window to answer some final questions. The three officials on the other side of the window stared at Ben and me for a few moments. Suddenly one of them held up a copy of *The New Yorker* and all three of them smiled and gave us the thumbs-up. What a moment! With tears streaming down my face, I jubilantly acknowledged their approval. The *New Yorker* episode was just one of many challenges we would face as a new family.

I called the early intervention group that I had used for many of my adoptive families in Manhattan. The therapists came one after another to evaluate the developmental milestones of this now butterball baby boy. He couldn't keep his head up straight, he still held his hands in fists, and he wasn't able to turn over. He qualified for services with an occupational therapist and a physical therapist because his delays were 33⅓ percent in each domain of development, that is, gross motor and fine motor.

I didn't know what to expect, even with all of my experience with adopted kids. Still, we settled into our family life. This was my kid and there was no map or predetermined plan. We just hoped that with all this work, he would be okay, whatever that meant.

Ben had six hours of physical and occupational therapy a week, but then, at ten months, he let out his first belly laugh and we came running to witness it. His neck had straightened over the months with a lot of manipulation, massage, and hard work on his part. He was happy in his Boppy pillow, able to see the world around him. He finally walked at fifteen months with a great sense of pride in himself. But his thumbs hardly ever came away from his palms. He grabbed everything with his fingers alone. The therapists frankly were baffled and finally suggested little braces, which were useless.

What was most encouraging was his ability to communicate. He vocalized constantly right from the beginning so those parts of his brain appeared to be very active and intact. And language came swiftly for him. While his body failed him in some ways, he was content and so were we. He could enjoy intimacy and social connections because he could understand us and make himself understood. As I see it, Ben had a gift for communicating. Many of the kids I see in my office struggle for years to communicate and are terribly frustrated.

After five years of occupational therapy and handwriting

tutoring, Ben had his thumbs back and was able to write letters and numbers indistinguishably from other children his age; in fact, he was quite adept and became a Lego master, a cello player (with a kid-sized cello, of course), and he now plays the piano. Today Ben is a very happy and healthy boy, and both Diana and I think his fingers are very pretty and magical when he plays the piano.

As an adoption medicine specialist, I have traveled all over the world visiting orphanages and learning about the many facets of "orphanage society." I wanted to know why the children who arrived in my office from institutions abroad looked through me and didn't shed a tear as I drew their blood and administered vaccines; I wanted to know why some of these sweet little ones often appeared limp and lifeless when offered intimacy or closeness. And I wanted to know why dear babies who were alert didn't attempt to vocalize. As I examined newly adopted children in my pediatric office, I observed children staring at their hands and lifting their legs into the air as if they had never realized that they could move these appendages; I realized that they were truly unaware of their physical place in the world. They had no understanding of their bodies and they knew nothing about what they could do physically.

As infants, many orphans around the world lie in cribs soiled and vanquished. Often they lie on their backs with bottles propped for their feeding, missing out on the experience of intimacy with a primary caretaker who holds, touches, and talks to them— the building blocks for attachment. As toddlers, they stand along railings, rocking side to side, cruising unsteadily along the railings of their large pens in soundless rooms. Nevertheless, children are amazingly resilient and—with the support of loving parents who are able to accept that the process can be very gradual and full of uncertainty—they eventually adapt and stabilize in their new home environments. As the testimonies in this section of the book reveal, the creation of a family through adoption can involve many challenges, but love and permanence are powerfully healing forces.

MELISSA FAY GREENE

Melissa Fay Greene is an award-winning author of five books of nonfiction, including Praying for Sheetrock, There Is No Me Without You, *and* No Biking in the House Without a Helmet, *and the mother of nine.*

THE SCIENCE OF HAPPINESS

In every decade, parents are surrounded by hype and anxiety. *Don't make mistakes! Don't screw up the kids!* But parents ought to be growing more relaxed rather than more panic-stricken, as the latest news from the geneticists is: "It's all genetics!" The nature/nurture debate is over! Nurture lost! Identical twins separated at birth and located thirty-five years later will present themselves to researchers as matching curly-haired AP biology teachers in size 9 shoes and capris, living in midwestern states, one married to a man named Steve and the other to a man whose middle name is Stephen, and they both raise dachshunds!

Adopted, biological: it makes no difference. A one-out-of-a-hundred-billion twist of DNA, slotted into place at the moment of conception, plots a child's course.

Except for one thing. According to the scientists, parenting seems to make a difference in a person's sense of optimism.

If that's the only bone they're tossing us, I'll take it. Happiness, hope, and a can-do spirit can wreak miracles.

. . .

One of our sons by adoption arrived in Atlanta from Addis Ababa in the summer of 2007 at age thirteen. A tall and gloomy fellow, he'd seen a lot of the worst that life can offer: a loving family splintered by HIV/AIDS, displacement from his village to an orphanage in the city, almost everything he'd known washed away. When, in our kitchen, his long narrow face lit up with laughter, it was a wonderful sight. But it was a brief one. His expression soon fell back to distaste. His first clearly enunciated English phrase was: "Oh my God."

"Oh my God" meant: this is a total disaster.

. . .

One afternoon that summer, I came home from the market and found him sitting on a blue Adirondack chair in the front yard, within the lacy shadows of the Japanese maple. He was curved into a posture of grief, cradling his face with his long-fingered hands.

"What's wrong?!" I cried, setting down paper sacks of peaches, corn, and onions.

He looked up and said, "My life, oh my God," and returned his face to his hands.

"What's wrong with your life?"

He looked up again with haggard eyes. "Helen," he said, naming his new younger sister, an ebullient and sparkly girl of eleven, "will *not stop laughing.*"

Contemplating where he'd been, the bleak future that had

loomed before him, and the opportunities that spread before him now, I couldn't think of a reply. I regathered the produce and went into the house. "He's not used to the presence of a lighthearted girl," I thought. "Even the sound of feminine laughter rubs him the wrong way." Later I considered that the sound of merriment itself, regardless of gender, offended him as untrue. Laughter did not strike him as one of the world's authentic sounds.

And he bore grudges; he could nurture a small kernel of resentment for months. His bony shoulders seemed knotted with strife. He was an athletic boy, but his movements were jittery rather than lithe. From afar, you might have thought you were seeing a vexed middle-aged man in a hurry, the bony elbows pumping, the face slightly averted in preparation for bad news.

Then it was time for his first-ever science project in his first American middle school.

As the mother of nine, I've done more than my share of science projects. Not only have I wrestled home the tall three-paneled backboards and the stick-on letters, but I've been there beside the seedling that withered and the seedling that grew, the bread scrap that produced mold and the bread scrap that produced even more mold, the pea plant that listened to Mozart and the pea plant consigned to silence.

Our new son's science project happened to be assigned when articles about positive psychology, the "science of happiness," appeared in the news. Beginning in the 1990s, psychologists like Martin Seligman and Mihaly Csikszentmihalyi wondered why their field focused heavily on mental illness and depression. Why not study happiness, they asked, and strategize with people to increase their portion of it? I proposed the science of happiness to my grumpy son. *Okay*, he shrugged. He knew nothing of Mozart and pea plants anyway.

Together we researched and assembled the words for his paper. "There are things that people believe lead to happiness, but scientists say they do not lead to happiness," he/we wrote. "The first is money. For poor people, money can increase happiness. For middle class and above, happiness does not increase with more money, not even from winning the lottery."

Together we learned that the path to happiness is lined with friends, family, and experiences rather than with objects, even the most expensive luxuries. "If you are choosing between jewelry and a trip to the beach, start packing!" We learned that DNA accounts for no more than half a person's disposition—or "set point"—and that individuals can raise their set points.

I didn't know if my son had been born pessimistic, or if the tragedies of his young life had shaped him. But I watched him absorb these studies with keen interest. "You can't just decide to be happier one day and instantly become happier," he wrote. "You have to practice. One exercise is named 'three blessings.' Every day, write down three things that went well and you will feel less depressed three months later and six months later . . ."

"In conclusion," he wrote, "to become happier, a person should think of good things, have good friends, spend good time with his family, and be grateful for what he has."

He shyly presented this material to his class and was startled by applause. He/we got an "A"! Two years later, in ninth grade, he revisited this subject in more depth and felt validated again by an

"A" and by the interest of his classmates. By then I believe he'd begun practicing what he preached.

. . .

One night last week, my tall and relaxed eleventh-grade son unexpectedly joined me on an evening walk around the block. There was something on his mind. At six foot one, he amiably slowed his pace to allow me to keep up. "Mom," he said, "I am deciding what to be in life." We'd discussed this recently in preparation for a visit to his high school advisor. "I want to be the person who helps other people to feel happy. What is that name?"

"Well, psychologist, or counselor," I said.

"Yes. Last year a boy from school killed himself, you remember? He was sad because his girlfriend dumped him. I want to be the person who tells him to be happy, not kill himself. I can do this? This is a job?"

"Yes, it's a job," I said. *Oh my God*, I was thinking.

Not *Oh my God* as in *This is a total disaster.*

Oh my God as in *Parents do matter. Look what we have done together.*

MEREDITH KENDALL VALDEZ

Meredith Kendall Valdez lives outside Nashville, Tennessee, with her husband, Miguel. They brought home their son, Shafer Eyob Hailu Valdez, from Ethiopia in March 2012. Fruition is a beautiful thing.

Adoption was placed in my heart long before my husband, Miguel, and I met in high school. As it would be, it was placed in his heart as well. In September of 2008, I asked him at dinner what he thought about adopting our *first* child. He replied immediately, "Sure, we can adopt first." After one tender year of marriage, it was a moment I knew would shape and define our lives. We joyfully began our paperwork in August of 2009.

Along the way I came across Melissa Fay Greene's book *There Is No Me Without You*, an important account of the AIDS orphan crisis in Ethiopia. It so completely bent my thinking that I encouraged Miguel to read it as well. Around this time Miguel, an avid mountain biker, lost his wedding ring one day on the trail. We had the ring insured but discovered that the amount we received would not cover replacing the exact ring. Miguel finished the book one evening and came downstairs and said, "I want to get a less expensive ring and donate the difference to AIDS babies." (Did I mention that he is precious?) Having heard of "the orphan doctor," we came across the Worldwide Orphans Foundation website and read about Des's Village in Ethiopia. In late 2010 we donated $923.39 to WWO, the difference between the cost of the new ring and the insurance payment. When the new ring arrived, I asked Miguel what we might engrave on it. Without missing a beat, he replied, "AIDS babies."

On an otherwise ordinary day in June of 2011, we received a call that there was a little boy . . . for us. Our hearts stopped beating as we saw pictures of Setota for the first time. It is the moment adoptive parents, long into their paper pregnancy, dream about. All of the plans and preparations in motion solidified in his image. Two months and three days later something unusual happened. We learned that we would not be this child's parents. We were told it would feel like a death, and it was. Raw, we struggled to reconcile our feelings of loss.

Four days after the news came about Setota, we received another referral, and he was a gift named Eyob Hailu. In the photos, he looked at us with worried eyes. His medical records were complex and we asked our physician to help us ascertain their meaning. She e-mailed "the orphan doctor" herself, whose foundation, Worldwide Orphans, was responsible for his medical care in Addis Ababa, Ethiopia, the same foundation we had donated the ring money to months prior. In awe of the connectedness, we accepted our second referral with peace and great anticipation. Months later, we traveled to Ethiopia to meet Eyob Hailu. Our time together was inexplicable perfection and beyond what our hearts dared to hope. We now wait, bursting at the seams, to travel a second time to bring our child home.

What we have learned about adoption thus far is that a child on the other side of the world whom you may have yet to meet, who doesn't look like you, and who may not even speak your language, can bless and inform your life in immeasurable ways. There are countless children around the world who are born into unthinkable circumstances and hunger for love, hope, and deliverance.

Our journey serves as a poignant reminder that each of these children is real and individual, not part of a critical mass too sizable to serve and protect. Each has a little face that smiles and cries, little hands that grasp and pray, and a little heart that feels and needs. To us, Setota has become the face of all the world's vulnerable children, challenging us to see those who are so often overlooked. Some of the greatest lessons are the most painful to learn.

Moreover, we have learned that our capacity to love cannot be tethered. I struggle to wrap my mind around what a great privilege it is to love, mother, advocate for, and educate Eyob Hailu, victorious healer of our rather wounded hearts. He was sent to us on purpose as a gift we are ever humbled to receive.

Photograph taken by Kristine Neeley.
Shafer (Eyob Hailu) Valdez with his adoring parents, April 2012

STEPHANIE BAKAL

Stephanie is a writer and documentary filmmaker. She lives in New York City with her husband and two children, who were born in Vietnam.

DO YOU LOVE ME TOO, MAMMA?

"Tell me," they'd say. "It was love at first sight, right?"

When my son was placed in my arms as a baby in Hanoi, I fell head over heels.

This time, everything was different.

The first time I saw my daughter was on the Internet. Peering out from the "Waiting Children" section of an adoption agency's website were an infant with webbed toes, a toddler with a cleft palate, and older kids tainted simply because blood from HIV-positive mothers ran through their veins. Given the chance, any of them could probably grow up to lead happy, healthy lives.

She was standing in her metal crib. Three years old, brown eyes staring from the computer. "You want me?" she seemed to dare. "Take me, I'm yours."

I spent boundless amounts of energy trying to persuade my husband that this was the right thing to do. "Can we handle an older child?" he'd fret. It wouldn't be easy, I knew, but I couldn't get her out of my mind. "How can we not?" I'd reply. I called the adoption agency to say we'd take her.

In the months it took to complete our paperwork, we studied

photos of her for clues of her burgeoning personality. Affectionate and curious. Sometimes a vacant stare.

I couldn't wait to bring her home and love her. We studied Vietnamese and made a photo album to send her. Our six-year-old son began imagining life with a sister, rearranging his room, picking out toys, choosing her dresses.

"Mom?" he'd ask. "When she's here, will there be enough love left for me?"

"More," I'd say. I was flying blind. Virtual family. Made on a Mac.

When the agency called, we had less than a week to get to Vietnam. Thirty hours, ten thousand miles, a quick shower, and a bowl of chicken *phò* later, we were headed for the orphanage on the outskirts of Saigon.

We pulled into the courtyard and there she was.

Tiny but tough, she stood barefoot among a dozen kids dotted with odd purple stains, like strange mythical creatures. "Chicken pox," they told us. I took her in my arms and introduced her to her brother and father.

Poised and charming, she kissed my cheek, dutifully pronouncing *"Mẹ"*—"Mother." Taking our hands, she led us around the playground and the room where she slept, bravely welcoming us into her world.

Beaming, my son whispered, "I think she likes us."

By the next day, her demeanor had changed. Clutching the photo album, she hung back, sad and fearful. Realizing she was about to leave the only world she'd ever known, she became hysterical, putting up such a fight I had to remind myself that this was an adoption, not a kidnapping. The kids reached for her, convulsing in tears. *"Chào em!"* "Little sister, bye-bye!" She vomited all the way to the hotel.

Two hours later, she was splashing in the pool, eating French fries, and throwing pillows at her brother, their laughter filling the air. But at the end of the day she wanted to go home to the orphanage. She ran naked to the door to put on her shoes. She trusted only her Vietnamese-born brother to comfort her, feed her, and sing her to sleep. We awoke the first night to find her sitting upright in her cot, looking around in a panic. We were still strangers. I didn't go to her, afraid it would upset her. Helplessly, I watched until finally she lay down, thumb in mouth, and fell asleep.

Back in New York, picnics, walks on the beach, and playdates were derailed by visits to doctors, labs, and more doctors. Her belly was distended, muscle tone low, ribs bowed by rickets, and teeth badly decayed. She needed general anesthesia, a root canal, and five stainless-steel crowns.

She spent four years in an orphanage. We knew there would be developmental delays. What caught us off guard was having a four-year-old and a toddler rolled into one. Fiercely independent (she dressed herself, ate with chopsticks, and kicked a soccer ball like nobody's business), she wanted to explore her new world. But her language delays—even in her native Vietnamese—made her easily frustrated. She was given to tantrums, often throwing herself down in the middle of Broadway when things didn't go her way.

At school and in speech therapy, she was resilient and hardworking—an Eliza Doolittle transforming rough-hewn Vietnamese into intelligible English. At home she was a tyrant—stubborn, manipulative, and a drama queen. Playdates were a challenge. With limited language skills, sharing was hard to negotiate. One moment she'd be happily playing or singing Vietnamese songs. The next she'd be dazed, staring into space. Some days she'd wake up crying with a faraway look in her eyes. Others, she'd regale us with her lusty laugh and irreverent antics.

I became short-tempered and irritable, not just with her but with my husband and son as well. After one grueling day, my son looked at me forlornly and lamented, "She's not as much fun as I thought she'd be, Mom. Can't we send her back? She's killing us." Secretly I had to agree. I was guilt-stricken that love wouldn't come. I wasn't a mother—I was a drill sergeant. Exhausted and depressed, I felt shut out from the rest of the world.

She began to look like a regular New Yorker. Crossing Broadway in polka-dot sunglasses, pigtails bouncing, she'd wave and blow kisses to everyone from gray-haired ladies to guys whistling at her from motorcycles.

"I love you!" she'd tell her dad. And the taxi driver too. When we'd go out to eat, she'd enjoy embarrassing me with wicked parodies of my most unflattering self. "Don't you ever, ever, do that!" she'd rant in her Vietnamese accent, finger wagging crossly, just like mine. The speech therapy was beginning to pay off.

One day, at home with a cup of tea, I felt her hand on my arm, her eyes full of concern. "Mamma, you tired?" Her empathy was disarming. In that moment, she stole my heart.

Our son still won't admit to liking his sister but will ask, "Mamma, can she sleep in my bed tonight?" and I let them giggle longer than I should before reminding them that it's way past their bedtime.

The other morning, my son climbed into my bed to cuddle. "I love you, sweetheart" came naturally from my lips. My daughter stood spying on us in the doorway.

"You love me too, Mamma?" she whispered.

I invited her in and told her I did.

KIM BUSH

Kim lives in Morristown, New Jersey, with her husband, David, and their two sons.

Our first post-placement interview, about three months after our return from Kazakhstan, was a throwaway. Basically, the social worker arrived and documented that our newly adopted twelve- and thirteen-month-old sons from two different orphanages in Uralsk, Kazakhstan, were alive and well and had survived the journey from the land where they were born into "real" life. Six months later, she arrived again, and after listening to our update and seeing the results of love, good nutrition, and TLC, she proclaimed: "Your boys are attaching so well!" Whatever that meant—I just wanted her out of my house as quickly as possible. Her presence made me uncomfortable for a reason I couldn't identify. I filed her comment away in my brain while simultaneously ushering her out the door and scurrying off after our two toddling boys, who had scattered like cats. Once she left, that familiar feeling of discomfort returned as I pondered her exclamation.

I had been told that Deborah Gray's book *Attaching in Adoption* is a must read for any adoptive parent. During my paperwork pregnancy, I heeded the advice of other adoptive parents and bought her book, along with about a dozen others; I skimmed it, circled a few things, and put it on a shelf. At that moment, knee-deep in documents that required apostilles (a certificate that legalizes a document for use in another country) and frustrated with the bureaucracy of adoption, I found that Gray's book didn't resonate with my empty heart. That book didn't belong in the home where my husband and I had methodically prepared the room with two cribs for both our baby boys. Attachment, I rationalized, was just another phase scheduled to occur between our court date in-country and passport acquisition. It would conclude as soon as the four of us boarded that plane for Frankfurt. Our journey would be different, and once home, our babies and their immediate connection to us would change that house which was void of the type of love and contagion that children bring.

In a matter of months, our family expanded and contracted, both physically and emotionally. We lived closely in small rooms, charting measurable progress as both successes and failures. We made noise while trying not to disturb each other. We did our daily "things" while trying to stay quiet. We coexisted in that space while trying to resume our lost independence. We tried to meet our own needs, the needs of each other, and the needs of the helpless little people we had brought into our home. We moved throughout each day but were really just barely surviving this delicate balancing act, this storm of emotions and feelings that seemed to build and never subside no matter how hard we tried.

Then I got sick. At first we attributed my fatigue to the adoption process itself, and then to the demanding needs of our two toddlers. The illness had really been a slow, misdiagnosed spiral that began several years prior to our adoption journey. And while caring for our two boys was a contributing factor, it wasn't the cause of my illness. Soon the small rooms of our home became even smaller as they filled with mail-order pharmacy supplies and durable medical equipment. Visiting nurses came and went during all hours, on sunny days and rainy days, and even on holidays, those occasions that are supposedly joyous, meant especially for children.

I lived on the sofa, with my arm attached to an IV line delivering medicine that would make me sicker at first and then (hopefully) well soon after. Our boys grew quickly during this time, and I observed how their personalities changed while I rested on the couch. They approached me tentatively. They tried to cuddle and hug me but accidentally pulled out my IV instead. They were happy and scared. They had so much energy, and I had so little. They played together quietly and nicely, then fought and acted out their anger on each other, their father, and themselves.

Our boys experienced their own growing pains during this time, which turned into issues requiring more help than we as parents could provide. There were issues that arose for each boy independent of the other and issues specific to the sibling relationship that required us to make additional decisions and changes regarding their care. During this upheaval we tried to keep their lives and daily routine as normal as possible, and our boys, always as a pair, spent a great deal of time with close friends and relatives while I tried to get well.

Soon we needed to be reacquainted. Our group of four, now with different needs, had a new idea of "normal." In the throes of illness, I viewed our lives as stagnant, but change crept in. Life moved on, and we adjusted. More holidays passed, and we even made it through a few stable weeks without medical intervention before being besieged again. Medical intervention seemed to come and go with each season. Summer arrived and we played, and healed, and made the best of our situation. Love and support of one another and from others helped guide us through.

When our oldest son began kindergarten, we all four walked up the driveway to wait together that first morning. The bus arrived, and our oldest son hesitantly climbed aboard, paused for a moment, and then turned to cry into my leg. After watching the bus move a distance down the street, we turned to walk back to the house. Only one of us, our youngest son, was still at the top of the driveway waving to the disappearing bus, which carried his brother away from him. Then he began to weep inconsolably and uncontrollably, sobbing to us that he missed his brother so much, and asking us if he would ever return. The neighbors who witnessed this scene called us to make sure that we were okay. Once in the house, we all three began to weep, and wondered how we would make it through our first day of kindergarten. We parted ways, and did make it through that day, as well as the subsequent weeks of autumn and long months of winter that followed. Now we are enjoying the freshness of spring, which little boys and their rain boots adore.

Looking back on these past years, I understand at last what the social worker meant that day. Our group of four is still attaching— together, apart, separately, and to one another. We're attaching in ways that defy illustration. More important, it continues. I have thought a lot about the significance of attachment these years, and keep meaning to find Gray's book to explore it further. I have longed to discuss attachment with other parents but find that my friends with biological children don't have a clue what I'm talking about. Yet I know that we four separate beings today are together attached as a family. These days, I keep quiet and beam internally with pride at the progress we've made.

JOHN AND JUDY DEMARINO

John DeMarino is a retired executive from JPMorgan Chase,
where he worked for thirty-seven years. His wife, Judith
DeMarino, has been an executive manager with Hewlett-
Packard Company for twenty-seven years.

Judy and I made a decision to adopt a child sixteen years ago. We
met with Dr. Jane Aronson, who helped us through the process.
We chose to adopt a child from Russia because Judy's grandparents had migrated to the United States from Russia. Our baby was
in an orphanage in Yekaterinburg, Russia.

We adopted Sara when she was seven months old. Writing our
thoughts down for this story brings back all the memories of the
process as if it happened last week. Traveling to Russia was exciting, however our eyes were opened when we arrived in Yekaterinburg and saw the poor conditions of the roadways. The orphanage
was an old building and lacked colorful flowers and green foliage.
Even the airport was austere and operated more like a military
facility with armed uniformed staff at every entrance.

Yekaterinburg is a rural area of Russia very near the border of
China. We had interpreters/facilitators who guided us and were
with us every day. The process to meet with the many Russian
government agencies for the adoption took almost two weeks. We
had to be patient and wait to be called by each agency.

The interpreters handled the distribution of gifts and additional fees that were needed to get us through the process quickly.
The orphanage was clean but sparsely decorated. It was very

apparent that the women doctors and nurses really cared for these children and many times sacrificed their own needs and salaries to ensure the children had the bare necessities. We would always meet our prospective seven-month-old daughter, Sara, in a specially decorated room with a few toys set up just for prospective parents. We would play with her for a few hours and then the staff would take her behind closed doors until we could meet her again the next day. We learned later that the children were dressed up especially for these visits and that when the visit was over they were placed in a large crib with multiple children and were dressed in a simple cloth wrap with no diaper (because diapers were scarce) to minimize their movement in the crib.

We were very apprehensive to proceed with the adoption when we were provided with medical reports indicating that Sara had several medical issues. We spoke over the phone with Dr. Aronson multiple times, and she explained that the Russian medical reports were created to fit a system called "defectology." She further explained that this includes medical terminology that is not found in American medical textbooks, such as perinatal encephalopathy. The terms were frightening and hard to understand. This system was found in Russia and Eastern Europe, and the reports were routine and not based on much science or substantial medical evidence for each individual child. All Russian adoption medical abstracts included some of these terms, and interpretation was challenging. Unfortunately, we couldn't get any health history on her birth parents. This is usually not available in orphanage medical records.

We knew that Dr. Aronson would help us work through any medical challenges we might face, and with our help Sara would have numerous opportunities and support that would never be available in her current environment. We made the final decision to proceed with the adoption and brought Sara home to the United States.

Once we were home, we brought Sara to multiple doctors to be tested and evaluated. When she was twelve months old, an MRI confirmed Sara had a mild case of cerebral palsy. We still continue to bring her to a variety of doctors and therapists so we can help her to reach her potential. Sara's motor coordination has developed slowly. She started walking at two years old, wore leg braces until she was eight years old, and had tendon lengthening surgery to help with her gait. At fifteen she still walks with an uneven gait, but this hasn't stopped her from taking dance lessons since she was three years old and playing sports.

EARLY MEMORIES: SARA'S CHILDHOOD

At ten to twelve months of age, Sara enjoyed jumping in her bouncy seat and riding on her rocking angel fish. She loved being in a swing, going back and forth for long periods. She liked to sit at the piano and hit the keys. Her first words were "Mommy," "Daddy," and then "bye-bye." Sara loved to go out with us to restaurants and was able to feed herself with a fork and spoon.

At three years old she knew what she wanted to wear and would cry if her mother put on sneakers when she wanted her party shoes. Today, at age fifteen, she's still stylish and has multiple pairs of shoes. Sara loved to be cuddled and held and told that she had done a good job. She was, and still is, strong-minded and strong-willed. She always wanted to do everything herself without assistance.

Throughout the years Sara has received physical and occupational therapy, but she's been mainstreamed in school. We're very proud of her accomplishments. She's now a freshman in high school, and she's always been a good student and achieves good grades.

Her first love, though, is dance. Since she was three years old she's gone to a dance studio, where she takes classes three times per week. She loves the yearly recitals when she can go onstage and dress in dance costumes. This is great physical therapy for her and improves her self-esteem. She's still playing organized sports like softball, soccer, basketball, and cheerleading in the Glen Cove youth programs. We have shelves full of her trophies for dance and sports activities.

Raising a child with physical challenges is heart-wrenching because we experience all her frustrations and try so hard to do what's needed to help her. On the other hand, Sara has brought special meaning into our lives, and we cherish the warmth, love, and affection she gives us every day. Strong family bonds have grown between her and her eleven cousins, her older brother and sister, her aunts and uncles, and us. We love her so much and will continue to support her in every way we can to ensure that she has a meaningful and happy life.

DIANA LEO

Diana has three children, a twenty-four-year-old daughter and two sons aged fourteen and twelve. All her children were adopted. She lives with her partner and sons in New Jersey. Diana shares the story of adopting her first child on page 108.

Among the many deep and powerful things that having a child teaches is that babies are a community enterprise and everyone seems to have a say in how you raise your child. When that child is adopted, people seem even more curious and less able or willing to self-censor.

I adopted my first daughter domestically. She was a healthy infant, born at the end of November during a particularly cold winter. I'd spend about forty minutes getting her dressed (diaper, onesie, socks, snowsuit, mittens, hat) and getting her bag ready (more diapers, change of clothes, bottles, wipes) for a half-hour foray on the Upper West Side of Manhattan to pick up a few groceries.

Typical interactions would go like this:

I go into the butcher shop with the baby in her Snuggly on my chest. The grandmotherly lady in front of me in line turns around and with one look takes in everything I am doing wrong. "Can she breathe like that?" she asks me. "She should be facing out. She can't breathe like that." I tell the yenta that she's fine and avoid eye contact.

When it's my turn, the butcher listens to my order and responds, "Do you know what the temperature is out? How do you take a baby like that out in this weather? Does your mother know you have her out?" (Note: I am forty-two years old.)

I get my meat and leave.

Anyone who's had a baby is subject to this type of behavior, but what's truly remarkable is what happens when people know your child was adopted.

Some questions/comments we've all been faced with:

- Who's the real mother?
- Were her parents drug addicts?
- Why'd they give her up?
- Does she have brothers and sisters?
- Are you going to tell her?
- When are you going to tell her?
- Are you in touch with her parents?

I had one friend who suggested responding to questions like this by saying, "Why do you ask?" Few people could think of any reason other than they were just curious.

Of course, parents who adopt don't think about their children being adopted all the time. This was brought home to me one day when my daughter was about nine months old. I was pushing her in her stroller up the hill from the park when another stroller mom came up beside me. She asked how old my daughter was and remarked, "She looks big." Then the mother looked from my daughter's fair skin to my olive complexion and from her big blue eyes to my brown eyes and from her blond wisps of hair to my medium brown locks and my average height.

"Her father must be quite tall," the woman said. "Actually," I said, without giving it any thought because I just wanted to make it up that hill, "I have no idea what he looks like."

That was one budding friendship that died on the vine.

PATRICE M. JORDAN

Patrice is a consultant and financial analyst who lives with her son, Alec, in New York City.

Alec and I became a family on December 29, 2005, in Kokshetau, Kazakhstan. After having successfully petitioned the judge with the most important and nerve-wracking speech of my life earlier in the day, I changed out of my "finery." I picked up my bag with very warm clothes for Alec and headed to the baby house, along with our wonderful translator, Inna, our driver, Oleg, and a couple who was picking up their newly adopted daughter.

Once Alec was dressed in his new multiple layers because of the below-zero temperature outside, we said good-bye to the caring staff. It was late afternoon and time to begin our new life together. Alec and I were sharing a semi-attached "cottage" with a couple and their daughter, who was adopted a few days before. It was very fortunate for both Alec and me that this lovely couple were already experienced parents because I was a clueless new mom and terrified I would do something wrong and hurt him.

The baby house staff had told me that Alec slept through the night after an evening bottle. This was not exactly how it played out. After his bottle, a diaper check, and some rocking, I put him in his crib next to my bed. This was not a good idea! Alec started wailing, and because we were sharing the cottage and its semi-attached walls were very thin, I picked him up immediately. The wailing continued. I checked his diaper and he was dry. He didn't want another bottle, refusing the one in my hand. He wasn't too hot and he couldn't be too cold because any building connected to the city's central heating system was toasty day and night.

I wondered whether he was afraid of the dark. I turned up the lights. He was still wailing. I hoped that I wasn't the reason he was crying, because then we would have a really big problem. I tried holding him and started to sing, which is not my forte, but I was desperate. I thought playing some music might soothe him, but he still wailed. It was getting late and I was worried about Alec. As well as myself, our housemates and neighbors were exhausted after such an emotional day.

I was still singing "The Lion Sleeps Tonight," one of my favorites but apparently not one of Alec's, when I called my mom (now Alec's grandma) in Staten Island, New York. Alec wailed even louder as I begged for advice. Mom/Grandma suggested singing to him. I started shouting and then was practically crying too.

Alec Jordan, son of Patrice Jordan

"Thanks anyway, Mom. I'll call again soon." I became frantic that we wouldn't make it through this night.

I held Alec closely and paced the floor of our very cozy room. I tried a bottle again (with a different nipple, but that's another story). That helped a bit. I finally concluded that Alec did not sleep through the night after an evening bottle but instead needed to eat every three hours, 24/7. He loved to be held until he was sound asleep. I considered that maybe something was lost in the translation from Russian to English.

Alec, now six years old, loves to cuddle at bedtime, and I am grateful for this "problem."

MEG BODE D'ARIANO

Meg has two daughters, Lily and Grace, and is married to Carmine. She is a board member of Worldwide Orphans Foundation and a media relations and event production specialist to the hedge fund industry.

It's the summer of 1998. My husband and I are finalizing our plans to go to China to meet our Lily, the daughter we have dreamed of for so many years. Her Chinese name is Li Pei, and she's waiting for us in an orphanage in the town of her birth, Shangrao. A few weeks ago, we received a tiny picture of her and promptly made copies to share with family and friends. We carry her photo with us everywhere, and proudly prop her up on tabletops when we go out to eat. We became a family the moment we were matched with her, and we can't wait to go get her and bring her home.

It's just two weeks before the trip that'll change our lives forever. My phone rings in my office. It's the adoption agency telling me there's a problem with Lily. She's not "thriving." The news is shocking, and I wonder what they are talking about. They don't have much information other than that she's very small and thin and not putting on weight. They give us a choice about our adoption. We can consider a different baby, we can see two babies when in China and then choose one, or we can accept Lily, as planned. I am devastated.

I call my husband with the news. Could we parent a sick child? What if she has a long-term illness? Can we handle the responsibility? Worse yet, what would happen to her if we don't adopt her?

Lucky for us, we had met Dr. Jane Aronson, an adoption medicine specialist, known as "the orphan doctor," through our agency. We call her immediately. Jane listens intently. Her focus and her empathy are extraordinary. She insists that we come to her office as soon as possible.

It's the next day and we're with Jane discussing our dilemma. She's thoughtful and sweet, yet firm as she leans forward in her chair to speak to us. "Look at me," she says. "You don't know this yet, but you're already parents. Your instincts are strong, and you can figure this out." We realize that if we leave her in the orphanage, there will be little chance that she would receive the attention or medicine she may need. Jane helps us to understand that only we can make the decision ourselves. "Look into her eyes. If there's any spark, bring her home." She encourages us to call her when we are in China.

It's two weeks later, and we've traveled to China with twenty prospective parents to collectively adopt ten babies. We're in our hotel room, waiting for a phone call inviting us to meet Lily in a room down the hall. We can hear voices and footsteps in the corridor outside our room, and then we hear babies fussing and crying. We're nervous wrecks! Finally, the phone rings. We fly out the door and weave our way through a sea of our travel mates also meeting their babies. We spot Lily. There she is! My husband reaches for her first and pulls her close, hugging her for the first time. We look into her eyes. Fireworks! She's full of sparkle and personality. We're ecstatic. We take her back to our room, and the romance begins.

Fast-forward three years to 2001. We're back in China, adopting Grace—the baby sister who Lily longs for. Lily's a healthy, happy four-year-old now, and Grace's adoption, "well, that's another story."

REGINA MCDONALD

Regina McDonald works in clinical research and lives in the West Village in New York City with her daughter, Zoe Tizita.

My daughter had been home for four months on Mother's Day, which happened to be my birthday this year. It was a sweet coincidence. I also was born on Mother's Day forty-five years ago when my own birth mother made the courageous decision to place me for adoption. She was only sixteen and in school. Every birthday my mom says, "Say a prayer for the girl who gave birth to you because I'm sure she is thinking of you today, and every day." Someday I will be saying this to my Zoe. Being an adoptee helped me decide that adoption was the way I wanted to start my family. Also, being a single parent felt "right" and less complicated for me.

The process was hard. The endless months of compiling paperwork were daunting. At one point during the paperwork process I panicked and wondered if I was ready. Then I panicked thinking that if I slowed the process down and paused, my social worker would doubt my commitment and take me off the list. Thankfully, she was kind and understanding, and when I was ready, we picked up where I left off.

Then my dossier went in and so began the long twenty-three-month wait. It was difficult and fraught with anxiety as rumors of Ethiopia discontinuing adoptions for singles became a threat. Wait times got longer and longer. I tried to take advantage of the time and considered taking one more vacation since that might not be possible after the baby came home. Then I thought I should go out with friends and eat at restaurants more often because that wouldn't happen for sure once I had a child. Nothing practical gave me much solace. I have had enough vacations and dinners out, and I wanted my baby and our life to start.

I began to fear that it was all going to go awry and the program would close or singles would be refused the chance to adopt. Being adopted myself, my parents always spoke of God's hand in my placement and that we were destined to come together, to be a family. I tried hard to hold on to that belief. I tried hard to believe that my destiny was to be matched with my true child. I hoped that my destiny was not to be childless. It is tough when things aren't moving forward, and the fear keeps you up at night.

When I first met Zoe Tizita in Addis Ababa, Ethiopia, I stared and stared at her and honestly could not believe my luck. She emanates this light. She was hesitant, but at the same time she was sure of herself. She looked me in the eye and held my gaze. At fifteen months old she was serene. She was adorable. I was smitten.

When we got home to the United States, there were of course challenges. I never knew I could be so tired. She would cry inconsolably at bedtime until she exhausted herself. I was so afraid of traumatizing her by letting her cry because I thought that she had already been through enough. What if letting her cry "ruined" this gorgeous and delightful child?

We made it through. Friends have been amazingly supportive, but being the only parent can be lonely and scary. Zoe Tizita is an exceptional child. She is loving and bright and an active and curious nineteen-month-old. She loves to laugh and to chatter. She waves to say "Hi!" to all the people we pass when we walk down our street in the West Village of New York City. I am blessed to be her mother and I know it's harder and better than I ever imagined.

NANCY JO JOHNSON

Nancy Jo is a photojournalist and graduate student in New York City, working on a master's degree in social work. She lives in Westchester with her husband, Pfitz, and two children, Lhakdon and Norden.

"I believe you are a true freedom fighter," the Dalai Lama whispered to me as he embraced me in 1993. At the time, I was a photojournalist returning from a trip to Tibet, and I'd wept to him when I described the injustices visited on the Tibetan people by the Chinese occupation. But still, I didn't know then what it really meant to be a freedom fighter.

My apprenticeship as a freedom fighter began in 1997 when I met a group of orphans who had been resettled in a Tibetan orphanage in northwest India. For the next decade, I traveled to the Himalayas as a photojournalist and trek organizer, and I always made it a priority to visit the children. Each visit strengthened our bond, and it became harder to leave them. When I married in 2002, my husband and I began the arduous process of adopting a boy and his older sister from that group of orphans. Five years later our daughter joined us in New York; six months after that, her younger brother, our son, finally came home too.

I thought that was the happy ending of our tortured saga, and I had no idea that it was actually just the beginning. I didn't realize the extent of our son's behavioral and mental health issues. He was an active child who was smart, demanding, and moody. He had a sweetness that over many years of trauma and neglect at the orphanage had been shadowed. After he and his sister were separated at the orphanage, he was labeled a "bad" kid and beaten regularly for his inability to keep up with schoolwork. His anger deepened, and by the time he came home with us in the summer of 2007, he was a master of defying authority. At the young age of thirteen, anger was his weapon.

His darkness caused us all to become dark, and we became a family in crisis. Nothing in my past had prepared me for dealing with a child who'd been abandoned and abused. It was like taming a wild animal. We faced life-threatening violence, property abuse, daily stress, fear, and anxiety. I nearly lost my job as a photo editor at *Fortune* magazine. Life as we knew it ceased to exist, and life as we hoped it would be with our new family seemed a distant dream. During the first eighteen months, we had to hospitalize our son three times, and there were emergency room visits and police interventions.

Both children faced extraordinary adjustments. The cultural and language gaps were huge because they hadn't lived in a home with parental supervision since they were toddlers. They had very few nurturing adult figures in the orphanage with a forty-to-one ratio of children to adults. Our daughter assumed the role of mother to her brother and protected him as much as she could. For her too adults were figures to be outwitted. We had to peel back layers of trauma to tackle the bigger issues of honesty, trust, and attachment. The idea of therapy, which we explained as "doctors you talk to," was foreign to them. Our son kept saying he wasn't "sick." We needed to convince him that he was sick. We told him that we wouldn't give up on him or give in to the anger he used to control everything in his/our life. For us to survive as a family, we had to free him from his rage.

This traumatic process to help my children forced me to ask educated questions and understand a new vocabulary. When faced with getting our children the services they needed, we struggled to find the right psychologist, the right psychiatrist, and the right personal therapist for our son. We entered the crisis so quickly that one psychologist became our family therapist, with whom we began weekly parent training sessions. She recommended that our son attend weekly psychotherapy that utilized mood regulation, behavioral modification, distress tolerance, and anger management. It became clear that therapeutic and educational interventions would be required so that he could continue to make clinical gains and not deteriorate and regress. The rewards were never easy or fast, and often it seemed there would be no reward at all. It took nearly two years for positive movement to outweigh the turmoil.

Within the special education section of the Yonkers public schools, we were assigned an excellent social worker who helped us navigate the bureaucracy to get our son what was needed. He was first placed in a school that was like a day prison. There were guards at the doors, in the bathrooms and hallways. Our son still managed to run away twice, with no one figuring out how. Kids from the Bronx, Manhattan, Staten Island, and Westchester bounced off the walls, went to padded detention rooms, and got caught with knives. It was a scary place. Our home was like an institution too. There were rewards and consequences for everything. Behavioral charts became a second full-time job.

The turning point came when, at our wits' end, we looked into institutionalizing our son. Our family therapist presented this option to him with all of us together as a family. She told him we would always be his parents and that we would always love him.

She explained what hospital life would be like, which included that he would no longer have privacy, favorite foods, a bicycle, and his own computer. She told him that once he got better, he would come home to be with his family and all the things that he loved. In retrospect, he was quite shocked.

Finally, hints of improvement began, and we found the hope to persevere. He never had to go away. He settled down, and eighteen months later was given his second school placement, which was in a special needs school that wouldn't accept kids with behavioral issues. Presently, he is finishing his second year there, and for the first time in his life he loves school.

Our daughter was never volatile, but her coping mechanism was to bury the pain and go inward and lock herself there. We have slowly freed her from the role of caretaker, and the patterns between the siblings have begun to change. Initially she had no self-confidence and froze if placed in an unfamiliar situation. She has had intensive tutoring, sees a therapist regularly, and is attending a liberal arts college near our home on a full scholarship. She has extraordinary self-discipline, a terrific sense of humor, loves having a stable home, and is well on her way to becoming a most extraordinary young woman.

Living and working in the Third World inspired a curiosity about other cultures and influenced my openness to diversity. It gave me the ability to look at things from a different perspective, to deeply appreciate the gift of having enough food on the table, to understand the importance of family, and it inspired a confidence to challenge the status quo when it proved to be unfair. When I confronted obstacles with the adoption of our children from the refugee camp in India, not once did I consider giving up, nor did I regret the decision

I had made when confronted with the seemingly insurmountable challenges of settling our children.

My husband and I have had each other and our families. We believed that with time, patience, love, and the support of wonderful professionals, we would prevail. We still have a long

Lhakdon leaving Tibet, 1997

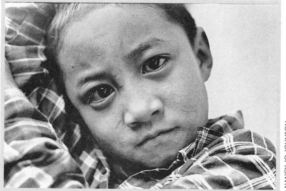

Norden, 1997

way to go, but what has happened to our family in the past four years has been an inspiration, not only to us but also to our extended families, our friends, and even our doctors.

The fight for freedom is not only waged on an economic and political level but on a personal level in the heart. The freedom to

Lhakdon and Norden, 1997

Pfitz and Lhakdon, 2010

love and be loved, freedom from fear and abuse, and freedom from anger and desperation are as important as political freedom. I will continue to work to the best of my ability to honor the compliment whispered in my ear by the Dalai Lama, one of the more extraordinary humanitarians of our time.

Left to right: Norden, Grandpa, Lhakdon, NJ, Pfitz, and Pasang (Lhakdon's good friend from Chicago), 2011

Norden, 2011

BRADFORD D. CONOVER AND
DEBRA SFETSIOS-CONOVER

Brad Conover is a civil rights attorney and his wife, Debbie
Sfetsios, is a children's book art director. They live with their
son, Bereket, in New York City.

As I approached age fifty, with my wife, Debbie, not far behind, we
set out to adopt. More than seven years later, the city passed by
our window in a numb sleepless blur as we raced from JFK back to
our five-flight walk-up apartment. Beside us was Bereket, age nine
months, from Ethiopia.

Our seven-year journey began in 2002 with Vietnam. More
than a year of paperwork and just one month after we had secured
the necessary U.S. government approvals, Vietnam closed all adoptions and never reopened during our approved eighteen-month window. China and a new adoption agency came next. About a year
into the process, China changed its age requirements, disqualifying
us from adopting. In 2007, we started from scratch for the third
time with a new agency and a country relatively new to international adoptions, Ethiopia.

About two years later, an e-mail appeared on my computer
screen at work. Attached was the head shot of a tiny baby and one
page of scant medical information indicating that his mother had
died of malaria a few months after his birth. In a photo, his eyes
were tearful, half shut, his skin was pale, and the corners of his
little mouth were down and twisted. His pajamas rested loosely on

diminutive shoulders. My experience with babies at that point was little more than seeing chubby smiling babies pictured on TV commercials. A second picture arrived, his big eyes again peering out above an even looser fitting red flannel shirt. The agency wanted to know if we wanted to proceed. We said yes.

We arrived at the orphanage in Addis four months later in August 2009. We were taken to a small windowless cinder-block room no more than twelve feet in diameter. Lining three walls of the room were cribs, two babies each, with one nurse caring for all in a twenty-four-hour shift. Seeing the other prospective parents happily bonding with their giggling new charges, we reached down to pick up Bereket. He looked away with that same pained expression we recognized from the photos.

Something was wrong. Our calls and e-mails to our agency back in the United States provided little comfort. The employee assigned to field such calls from anxious adoptive parents was well intentioned, but she might as well have been reading from a human resources manual. Our short visit with Bereket's father, two days later, in a small village in southern Ethiopia, was emotional but provided no new information that might explain Bereket's reticence. That night in a local hotel room lying under mosquito netting, I pictured Bereket back in his crib in Addis not wanting to be touched, avoiding eye contact, and never smiling. I panicked. What had we done? Had I made the biggest mistake of my life in talking Debbie into an adoption? Debbie listened to my fears. She said, "Don't worry, it will all be all right." Debbie had raised three children into adulthood from a previous marriage, one with a significant physical disability. I said, "Okay," but my heart was racing with fear.

We write this story nearly two years later. Bereket, a healthy two-and-a-half-year-old, is napping happily on an early summer afternoon. About a month after our return from Ethiopia, after repeated testing, Bereket was diagnosed with clostridium difficile colitis. We were told that antibiotics administered at the orphanage to treat repeated ear infections had likely stripped away healthy bacteria in his colon necessary to process nutrients. When Bereket turned away from us, he did so because his mind and body were in survival mode. He had been unable to retain nutrients. No matter how often he was fed, he was malnourished and slipping away, each month losing, rather than gaining, weight. We consulted with Dr. Jane Aronson, and that is how we discovered the cause of his sad expressions and weak physical state.

Under Dr. Aronson's care and the right medicine, the diaper changes became less frequent. Bereket's weight gradually stabilized, and then, beginning in January 2010, with each monthly doctor's visit, the numbers started to go up. The nine-month-old whose weight could not be found on the charts now is measured at

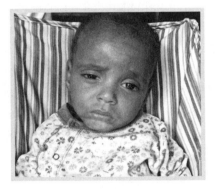

Bereket when he first arrived from Ethiopia

50 percent for healthy toddlers. Bereket's contorted and pained expression has given way to a contagious laugh, a prance in every step, and an irresistible charm. When the hectic pace of everyday life causes Debbie and I to neglect a good-morning hug, Bereket's little hands reach around and draw us together. He holds us tightly, and with the second language he already has picked up from his wonderful nanny, Angelica, he smiles at us and says, *"Familia."*

*Bereket with his mother, Debbie Sfetsios,
and his father, Brad Conover*

MARY CROTTY

Mary works in Manhattan and shares her life in Rye, New York, with Megan and her siblings Killian, Liam, and Maeve Harris and their dogs.

After a very long, arduous process with many ups and downs, we were finally going to meet our beautiful baby girl. We received pictures and updated videos of her from the time she was six weeks old, and she was turning one year old during our one-week visit. Her room was done, and she had a closet full of beautiful clothes. I'd researched the best crib, car seat, and every other item imaginable right down to the Diaper Genie. My dream of becoming a mom was finally happening. My husband and I left from JFK airport in New York to fly to Moscow. At the Marriott Grand we met several other American couples who were there to meet their children as well. We all set off for the Ministry of Education and Science to receive the "official referral," and then continued on to the baby hospital to meet our children. The excitement was building. We made arrangements to meet the other couples for dinner that night after we split up to go to different baby homes and hospitals.

Our adoption referral was a little girl named Marina, and she was at a baby hospital instead of a baby home, which meant she'd been in a crib and never removed since the time she was born. She was in a small room filled with five other cribs, where the children could see each other but not touch each other. All they had was the metal bars of their cribs and a mattress, and there were no toys or stimulation. There were several other rooms along the corridor with a similar setup of cribs.

When our interpreter took us down the road to the baby hospital, I was immediately shocked by the boarded-up doors of a building under construction. We climbed dark stairs with an awful stench that I will always remember. We knocked on a large door that was opened by a stern-faced caretaker who ushered us into a small office where we met the doctor. After a brief discussion, a caretaker brought this small baby dressed in several layers of old clothes into the room and handed her to me.

Marina started to scream and there was no calming her down. After a few futile attempts, my husband recommended that they put her back in her crib and we spend time with her in her own environment. I was so stunned by my surroundings. All of the screaming babies were trying to get our attention except our Marina. She wanted no part of us. She would just cover her eyes with her hands. I was sure she had something wrong with her. All I wanted to do was run. I was so overcome with sadness for these babies, and so upset by our meeting and lack of connection. How could I bring this baby home? Could I sacrifice my entire life taking care of a mentally challenged child? I insisted she have additional tests, all the while knowing that regardless of the outcome this was the baby that God wanted us to have, and we were going to bring her home.

That night after an emotionally draining day, and after finding out the good news that Marina was fine, we met the other couples for dinner, and I couldn't wait to compare notes. But when I heard mother after mother say how sweet their babies were and how they knew they were their children as soon as they saw them, I was devastated. I went back to our hotel room and cried my eyes out, realizing that I didn't have the same connection with my child. For the next four days my husband and I went to see Marina and had the same experience. Then my husband slowly got her to smile and do a head butt and I felt there was hope!

We went back to Moscow to pick her up and take her home to America a few weeks after our court appointment. After scrubbing her in the bath, washing her hair with baby shampoo, and putting on baby lotion, I dressed her in beautiful clothes and headed to the airport. She was starting to look like the baby girl I had imagined, but she was still wary of us. We had to give her Benadryl to make her sleep, and we laid her on a bed of blankets on the floor in first class because she would not let us hold her for very long. My goal was just to get her home.

After getting her home, Megan Maureen was welcomed by her grandparents, siblings, other family members, and dogs. She was showered with attention and was coming along slowly; we would get a smile here and there. After being educated about the importance of bonding so that Megan wouldn't think I was just another caretaker, my husband and I made the decision that only he and I would hold her, feed her, or change her for four months. All our loving friends and family and Megan's nanny would support us by cooking and taking care of the house, but they would not hold Megan. They interacted with her or played with her on the floor, but we were the only ones that took care of her needs.[1]

---

1. This practice is recommended by some social workers. I have always frowned upon this recommendation because there is no science to support the idea that this exaggerated approach will help the adopted child bond more quickly with his or her new parents. I have worked with thousands of families and I discourage the practice . . . but I understand why people do it. They are so frightened that if they don't do it their child will have reactive attachment disorder.—Jane Aronson

. . .

Fast-forward six months later: as many people told me would happen, I loved this child like no other. I couldn't imagine life without her. She was like a flower blossoming, reaching a milestone every day, rather than every few weeks like a typical child. She had a lot of making up to do and she wasted no time. With the assistance of Early Intervention (a health department program in our county), which included an occupational therapist, speech therapist, and a special education instructor, Megan quickly overcame delays caused by her lack of sensory stimulation. In addition to blossoming into a strikingly beautiful blond toddler, she had a smile and a personality that warmed every heart that she encountered. She entered school for two-year-olds the following September and hasn't missed a beat since. The joke in my family is that I worked too hard at bonding in the beginning, because Megan became glued to my hip.

She is now in kindergarten and is still warming hearts. As her kindergarten teacher wrote on her recent report card, "Megan blesses us with her giggly and joyful spirit and brings sunshine into our room every day." Academically, Megan is doing very well and is a popular child with a busy calendar. She loves gymnastics, ballet, jazz, ice skating, skiing, swimming, and most recently, tennis. As she rushes off to our club in her tennis whites for a lesson, I can't help but think of where she started and what she overcame. People say she is a lucky girl. We are the lucky ones. Since we met her, every Christmas has been merrier, every Easter and holiday has been happier, and every day has been sunnier. She may not have had me at hello, but she certainly has me forever.

Though not by our creation, Megan is our child by God's design.

V.

Becoming a Family

"Are you going to give me away?"

One day shortly after my son Des arrived from Ethiopia, he was in my car in the backseat on the driver's side while we were parked in front of our home, and before I knew what was happening, he opened the door and began to climb out of the car. He was nearly killed by a passing speeding car. I saw this disaster in the making in my mirror and like Elastigirl in *The Incredibles*, I reached back, grabbed him, and pulled him back into the car. He screeched and howled like a wild animal for a few minutes as I tried to explain what had happened. But it was useless, as he understood no English and was obviously traumatized by what had just taken place. I called my Amharic-speaking friend, Adey, and gave the cell phone to Des. They went back and forth for a few moments, and then, suddenly, he smiled. He understood what had happened. Though I knew well how complicated and scary it can be for children who have just been adopted to be living in a strange new country with a new family, I was shocked by this experience.

In the days and weeks that followed, I found myself becoming depressed from the heavy weight of the emotional work it was taking to help Des adapt. He had nightmares most nights and often responded frantically when we needed to leave the house, sometimes attempting to bar the front door with his body so that we all could not exit. As challenging and disturbing as this was, over time, our whole family rose to the task of helping Des feel secure and comfortable as a member of our family.

The essays that follow in this section pay tribute to the many special and unique ways that adoptive families establish themselves and evolve. An older child adopted from a poor country must learn a new language, try strange new foods—even visit a hectic American shopping mall for the first time. It is difficult for this child and his new family to fathom their cultural differences at first—but, with time, he becomes inextricably connected to his new family and his new life. A transracial adoption forever changes a family—and a community's—views on racism. When it comes to adoption, the formation of family demands an openness to explore the meaning of self, culture, family, community, and history, and the families in this chapter had the courage, humor, and humility to do so.

The epigraph to this section above is a quote from a twelve-year-old boy who was adopted from China by a single father. The father married a few years later, and then three other children were adopted from South Korea, China, and Russia. The quote—"Are you going to give me away?"—reveals how adopted children are constantly processing their identities—often when we least expect it. The father who heard these words from his son had to find special ways to reassure him that his place in the family was permanent. You may have heard the expression "forever family" in reference to adoption. The families in this section—though they oftentimes came from the far corners of the earth to find one another—are truly forever families.

CARRIE SUMAS

Carrie Sumas lives in Westfield, New Jersey, with her wonderful husband, Nico, and their beautiful and vivacious children Alex, Jack, and Ella. The Sumas family was thrilled to welcome Ella into their family when she was adopted from Taiwan in 2009.

OUR SWEET LITTLE VALENTINE

I've never been sure why it came up, but even before we were married, Nico and I had talked about adoption. We were both very lucky people who grew up in loving families. What about all of the kids in the world whose biological parents just couldn't take care of their children for one reason or another? Didn't it make sense to think about adoption?

As day-to-day life progressed in our twenties and our thirties, we traveled the path that most of our friends traveled. We finished our education, got married, and gave birth first to our beautiful fun-loving daughter, Alexandra Grace, in 2000 and then to our sweet happy-go-lucky son, Jack Nicholas, in 2002. Wasn't our family complete with two healthy children? We considered having a third but soon remembered our old conversations about adoption. Immediately the idea took root and began to grow. Nico and I had enough love to offer to a third child, and Alex and Jack would both love to have a little sister or brother.

By winter of 2007 we began investigating the adoption process. We immediately learned that the process would probably take at least two years, but we knew our baby would be worth the wait. Our lucky break came when a friend recommended we talk to Dr. Jane Aronson, who ended up being an invaluable asset as an expert on international adoption. Based on our concerns and specific set of circumstances, Dr. Jane recommended that we consider adopting a baby from Taiwan. She explained that Taiwan had a small adoption program and that one of its unique attributes was that it offered a foster-care system. This meant that our child would be living with a foster family and would receive a lot of one-on-one attention for the first few months of her life. Taiwan seemed the perfect solution for us!

All parents of adopted children know that the path to adoption is extremely emotional and exhausting. From the application forms, to the multitude of essays, to the numerous interviews, to the series of classes, the challenges just keep coming. The hardest part for us was keeping the adoption a secret. Alex was now about seven and Jack about five. Nico and I were having a hard enough time being patient. We knew that there was no way we could tell Alex and Jack that they would have a little sister or brother and then wait for almost two years. Except for the people who wrote our application recommendations and a few close friends, no one knew about our adoption plan. We just didn't want to risk someone slipping and revealing the adoption to Alex and Jack.

We did share our adoption journey with our dear friends, Cara and Jeff. Cara and I had met while I was pregnant with Alex and she was pregnant with her first, Marissa. Our girls ended up being born two days apart and have been best friends ever since. Two years later, Jack and their son, Jeffrey, were born five days apart and have a very tight bond. Three years later when Cara and Jeff had their third child, Grace, I felt a little guilty that we hadn't provided an instant friend for Grace. By the time Cara and Jeff's fourth, Theresa, arrived on June 17, 2008, we were well on our way through the adoption process.

We will never forget getting the news about Ella. We were on vacation in the Outer Banks of North Carolina eagerly awaiting news. While Nico was out for a walk with Alex and Jack, I took the opportunity to call our agency to see if there was any information. Our agency representative told us she had actually just sent us a photo and some information via e-mail a few minutes earlier. By the time Nico and the kids got back, I could tell by the exuberant look on his face that Nico had already picked up the e-mail on his phone. We couldn't believe how precious our little bundle looked. Her chubby cheeks, gorgeous eyes, and adorable spiky hair all looked so perfect. When we saw that her date of birth was June 18, 2008, I had chills. Our little one was born one day after Cara and Jeff's fourth child, Theresa. Our first kids were born two days apart, our second kids were born five days apart, and our youngest kids were born one day apart. To us it was a sign that not only had we gotten a wonderful little baby, but we had gotten the exact baby destined to be part of our family.

Our next step was to tell Alex and Jack. We can't imagine two kids being more excited. When they heard that our family would be adopting a little girl and saw her photo, they jumped and screamed and danced around and hugged each other! Alex and Jack could not have been more happy but had trouble understanding why we would have to wait before our baby could come home.

The next few months could not have been more exciting. All four of us waited for updated photos and news of our baby's progress. We used the time to get her room ready, buy clothes, and dig out some of Alex and Jack's baby toys. We later learned that Alex had prayed in church and promised to give up all of her Christmas gifts if she could get her baby sister home soon.

It was finally time to name our baby. We decided on Ella Jane Yi-Pei Sumas. Ella was for my mom, who had passed away several years earlier. Jane was for Nico's grandmother, whom we also lost a few years ago. Yi-Pei was the name given to Ella by her birth mother. For such a little person, Ella's big name fit her perfectly.

Finally, after two years of anticipation, Nico and I were allowed to travel to Taiwan to meet and bring home our new daughter. This would be our first time away from Alex and Jack for more than a single night. Alex and Jack weren't worried. They were excited to stay with their uncle Mike, plus we would be coming home with their little sister.

Nico and I arrived in Taipei a day early so we could have a chance to see Ella's birth country. On the second day of the trip, after a two-hour car ride to Taichung, we arrived at the home of Ella's foster family. When we first laid eyes on Ella, Nico and I melted. She looked just like her photos, and we immediately felt like she had been a part of our family forever. She looked so happy and healthy and was living in such a warm home with foster parents who obviously loved her. We knew Ella had a wonderful start to her life in Taiwan.

We spent an amazing few days in Taipei, which coincided with the Chinese New Year, while we waited for Ella's paperwork to be finalized. It was remarkable how quickly the three of us fell into step as a loving family. We were just missing two pieces of our puzzle and those were Alex and Jack.

We arrived home in New Jersey in the early morning hours of February 14. Every year since, Alex and Jack love to recount waking up early on the morning of Valentine's Day, hearing the cry of a baby, and racing down to meet their little sister. They screeched and hollered and carried on like we had never seen before. Immediately Alex and Jack, like us, were in love with Ella Jane Yi-Pei. Valentine's Day was the perfect day to start our lives together as a new family. On that day and ever since, Ella indeed has been our sweet little Valentine.

The Sumas children

LORI B. FINKEL AND ANDREW COGAN

Lori Finkel and Andrew Cogan live in New York City with their three children. Lori is the chair of the board of Worldwide Orphans Foundation and Andrew is the CEO of Knoll, Inc.

Aliyah (Hebrew for "ascent") Tamenech Cogan was born Tamenech Daniel in Shebedino, Ethiopia, on March 10, 2007. The journey from there to our home in New York City six months later is a testament to fortitude (mostly that of Aliyah's maternal grandfather), patience, faith, hope, endless paperwork, and fate. Aliyah completed our family and joined Andrew and me, big brothers Jed and Caleb, and even bigger Newfoundland Lulu, and opened our world to limitless possibilities and unlimited love. She is the greatest gift imaginable.

We started the adoption process about two years after our second son was born. I always wanted to adopt a child, having worked hard to achieve the freedom of some financial comfort and having always identified with the disenfranchised. Adoption seemed to make so much sense and it was also my dream. Fortunately, I have a partner who supports my dreams.

We decided to focus on Ethiopia. The physical beauty of the people and its land and their transcendent spirit, despite the senseless ravages of HIV/AIDS, poverty, famine, and corruption, called out to us. We aligned ourselves with a strong Semitic tradition with the Queen of Sheba and aliyahs from Ethiopia to Israel. The endless process began with the inside of every municipal building in New York City, and strangers (aka social workers) streaming through our home, interviewing our three-year-old son Caleb, and analyzing our financial statements, decor, contents of our refrigerator, and anything else that could be inspected. There were monthly updates from the adoption agency once we made the "list" of hopeful, yearning, impatient, would-be parents. We were all trying to be happy when others were matched, trying to understand why the government decided to shut down for months at a time, and trying to remember that all good things come to those who wait.

Although the process is a blur, there are a few memories that are imprinted in the Aliyah lore. My father-in-law's initial reaction of "Can't you just write a check?" clearly stands out. There is no better grandfather, and observing his patience as she rubs his hairless head and plays with his glasses is something. When we first were "matched" with Aliyah and received her "mug" shot, it was family meeting time. When I looked at her picture, I realized this was the same feeling I felt after each of the births of my sons. We belonged together. We would create traditions and memories and we would learn to love and live together. I needed Andrew and Jed to embrace our journey. Andrew and I had planned to bring Jed with us to pick Aliyah up while our younger son stayed at home. Jed told us that we were asking him to choose between his brother, Cal, and his new sister and that wasn't fair. He wanted to stay in New York City with his grandparents and cousins and meet his sister when his brother met her. We listened to Jed.

The memories of the trip to Ethiopia reverberate with the excitement and discomfort of new sights, sounds, colors, and the incredible anticipation of finally meeting our daughter. After our first meeting with her at the orphanage, we were so relieved that she was chubby and loved by the nannies and not nearly as scary-looking as her mug shot. I remember, as if it were yesterday, bringing Ali to the Sheraton, playing like crazy in our hotel room, watching her first giggle, putting her in the girl clothing I had been yearning to buy for nine years, and knowing that everything was going to be more than okay.

One of the most unforgettably funny images in Ethiopia was seeing white couples with their Ethiopian children strolling through the lobby of the Sheraton hotel in Addis Ababa. A shocking and painful image was my daughter's birthplace. We drove five hours south to where Aliyah was born and toured her family's two-room mud hut, where one room housed five people while a cow lived in the other room. It was in that mud hut that we attentively listened to the story of her birth. Her father died three months before she was born from malaria and her mother died a few days after she was born. I was, at this point in the story, hoping beyond hope that my malaria medication was working, while being eaten alive by mosquitoes. We experienced the unimaginable bravery, selflessness, and strength of her grandfather, who recognized that they could not feed Ali and hoped that she would become a strong and independent woman and would want to come back to Ethiopia to help.

I can't believe Aliyah just turned four years old. She's an old soul who is the rock of the household. Empathetic, hilarious, bossy, brilliant, and beautiful, Ali rules the roost and has opened up our lives to the most remarkable experiences. She tells her brothers to stop fighting and picking their noses, tames our latest canine beast, Elias, the one-hundred-pound Landseer, and is the loveliest friend, cousin, and granddaughter. Her drawings radiate a deeply rooted happiness and a sense of well-being with the biggest smiles and the most colorful rainbows.

Because we want to honor her homeland, Africa has become a huge part of our lives. Andrew and I were married two years ago in the Kalahari Desert (a long story) with the kids, my in-laws, Rabbi Greg from one of the few reformed synagogues in South Africa, and an African choir present. Next December we are returning to Cape Town for Rabbi Greg to preside over Jed's Bar Mitzvah, and then we'll travel to Kenya. Through this process, we've become involved with the international orphan crisis. I joined the board of Worldwide Orphans Foundation (WWO), and our family supports a program in Addis that sends orphans to day camp and sleepaway camp for a few weeks in the summer. This past summer my kids were junior counselors and campers at the day camp and they had the time of their lives. Even though we were not able to communicate via words, impenetrable bonds were formed through the universal language of play, humanity, and friendship.

I love watching our daughter search for her identity and where she belongs just like every other child. One day she'll appreciate the irony of our first trip to the American Girl doll store, where no matter how hard I pushed the Native American, Hawaiian, or "doll that looks like me," she refused to bring anyone home other than Rebecca and her Seder plate (Rebecca is the Russian Jewish doll). When I'm telling her a story and Ali doesn't know the person, she'll often ask in the same breath, "Are they brown-skinned? Are they Jewish?" While watching the recent royal wedding of Prince

William and Kate Middleton, she asked Andrew, "Where is the rabbi?"

We've lost the anonymity of the typical white Jewish family inhabiting the Upper East Side of New York City. People stare, trying to understand how we all fit together; sometimes taxicabs pass us by, alluding to the horrific undertones of fear and racism. As we exited a plane together, a little African American girl told Ali that Andrew couldn't possibly be her father because he's white and she's black. One mother at Jed's school was so uncomfortable when I showed up with Ali at pickup, that all she could say was how much Ali looks like Jed! All these moments are reminders that the road ahead won't be without its challenges, but we hope that Aliyah's strong foundation and integration into our family will see her through whatever biases and roadblocks the world may try to throw at her.

Finkel Cogan family at Camp Addis, summer 2010

Whether or not our beloved JAP (Jewish African Princess) Aliyah chooses to sit on Park Avenue and lunch, it is our sincere hope and belief that she and/or her brothers will return to Ethiopia and Africa to try and make a difference. We hope that we can reciprocate a fraction of the gift bestowed upon us—the gift of a little girl and the hope, humanity, faith, and universal goodness that she embodies.

STEPHANIE BAKAL

*Stephanie is a writer and documentary filmmaker. She lives in
New York City with her husband and two children, who were
born in Vietnam. This is her second story in the book.*

BLOOD MUST BE DRAWN

"I want it to be kosher," I told the rabbi. If we were going to do this,
I wanted to be sure that everyone accepted him as a Jew. If he'd
been born from my womb he would've been Jewish. Circumcised
or not. At his *bris* he would've been named "son of Mark and
Shulamite" (my Hebrew name). Because he was adopted, he would
have to be called by the names of the original Jewish patriarch and
matriarch. He would have to be "son of Abraham and Sarah," and
his new Jewish identity would not reflect our grandparents' names
and bloodlines nor his Vietnamese heritage. We wanted to do everything right and give him up fully to the Jewish tradition. What
if he were to fall in love with an orthodox girl? What if someone
told him he wasn't Jewish enough?

It was the Jewish New Year. In synagogue, I sat holding my son. I
looked down at him, his face like a Buddha, long almond eyes
wiser than his years. He did not have the blue eyes or curly hair of
my family that I'd imagined, passed down from my Eastern European Jewish ancestors. He did not have my husband's Roman

profile. Yet he was perfect and I felt complete. *"L'dor v'dor,"* I prayed. "From generation to generation."

Because he was already ten months old, we couldn't have the *bris* at home. So we found a surgeon who was also an orthodox *mohel* and scheduled a surgical circumcision at the hospital. The conversion to Judaism would take place at an orthodox *mikvah* where, after a ritual immersion, we'd receive a certificate of *brit milah* proving we'd fulfilled our covenant with God. We'd have a blessing and *kiddush* in the synagogue to celebrate. We were going to do everything right.

There was a fly in the ointment because our son ended up in the hospital with bronchiolitis. He was blue. They put him in an oxygen tent. I sat up all night making sure he could breathe, counting the "inhales" and the "exhales" until his rhythm returned to normal.

A few weeks later we thought he was well enough for the *bris*. We arrived at the hospital as instructed at six a.m. He was allowed only water in his bottle because he would need general anesthesia. The Asian anesthesiologist took one look at him and said, "I see he's been hospitalized for a bronchial infection. You realize that there's a risk he will have an asthmatic attack under anesthesia and a one percent chance of brain damage. He's here for an elective procedure. Are you sure you want to do this?"

Ten rounds of IVF. Two hearts that stopped beating. A 1 in 500 chance of Down syndrome. We had already played the odds and they were never in our favor. The *mohel* came into the OR and we told him that we couldn't go through with it. He did not try to change our minds.

When I called the rabbis and told them what had happened, they said, "Of course, any risk to the child must be avoided." I asked if instead of a *bris*, they could perform a *brit shalom* (or "covenant of peace"), which is similar to the ceremony that welcomes girls into the Jewish community. They told me that this was not the tradition, but that they would think about it.

I reached out to other rabbis and asked if there was any way our son could become Jewish without circumcising him. I was told over and over that according to the Covenant, because he was a boy, blood must be drawn.

I continued to go to synagogue. I'd hold my baby close, joyously dancing and singing "L'cha Dodi" to welcome in Shabbat. People came up to congratulate me and I would watch as families went up to the altar with their Jewish babies to receive their blessings. We were never called up for a blessing with our son.

Meanwhile, a family friend invited us to bring our son to the Abyssinian Baptist Church in Harlem on Martin Luther King Jr. weekend. There was going to be a baby blessing and we were invited to participate. We were welcomed with open arms by the congregation, no questions asked. When it was our turn to be called up to the altar, the Reverend Calvin Butts himself held our son up in the air and blessed him. And then we all sang "We Shall Overcome."

I was still waiting for my rabbis' decision on 9/11. I watched the towers turn to smoky flames; the clouds drifted uptown and lay heavy on us all. Suddenly, I felt vulnerable. I wondered if making my son Jewish would be a gift or a burden. What was this need to impose my Jewish heritage on my son? Was it for him or for me? Why did even a drop of blood need to be drawn?

When our son was eighteen months old, we were invited to a *bris* for our friend's eight-day-old boy. Our son took one look at the *mohel*'s carefully laid out knives and flung them onto the floor.

LISA SHAHAR

Lisa Shahar, co-owner and president of the website Adoption Under One Roof, and her husband, Ayal, raised three biological sons before they adopted their daughter, Ella, from Guatemala. They reside in the Midwest, where they are working hard to stay young to keep up with their daughter.

Each day when I pick up my daughter, Ella, from kindergarten, I am delighted to see her sweet little face among the crowd of children waiting for their parents. It is easy to spot her among the mostly Caucasian crowd of children because she has beautiful dark brown skin and long, straight shiny black hair. When she jumps into the car, the first words out of her mouth are, "Guess what we did today?" I am then promptly entertained with several minutes of stories from her day in kindergarten.

Before we adopted our daughter we were a family of five. Our three sons were thirty, twenty-five, and eighteen years old and the older two were married. Theoretically, we were getting ready to have an empty nest. That wasn't to be, because I desperately wanted to share my life with a daughter. It was not easy to convince the family that this was a good idea, but today none of us could imagine life without our little Ella.

Ella was adopted during the period that adoption from Guatemala was a swift and sure path. Guatemala was one of the few countries that allowed older parents to adopt children under the age of three. We were fifty-one years old when we submitted our paperwork to the adoption agency in September 2005. Three months later we received our referral, a precious five-pound baby girl. Although she was tiny, she looked perfect. One adoption doctor warned that her head circumference was too small and I should not accept the referral. My maternal instinct kept telling me that she was fine, but I wanted the reassurance from an adoption specialist. That was when I decided to contact Dr. Jane Aronson. First she explained that head circumference is notoriously not measured accurately abroad and is even a challenge for highly trained health care professionals, especially since babies can be moving targets. Then she mentioned the possibility of prematurity. She also discussed the differences in head size for different ethnic groups, keeping in mind that head circumference does have to meet certain standard criteria that may not exist in very poor countries like Guatemala. I am forever grateful to Dr. Aronson for the confidence she gave us in the decision we had already made to bring this little darling into our fold.

We brought Ella home at seven months of age, and for the next two years she was my entire world. My daughter was shy and did not like strangers, and during those two years she had little interest in anyone but me. We were a self-sufficient unit often oblivious to the outside world. We were bonding and we were in love. Having already lived fifty-two years, I knew that I wasn't missing anything. Gradually we left our cocoon and today Ella loves to socialize.

Is the love for an adopted child different than the love of a biological child? Not for me, and frankly, Ella is so lovable and kissable that even the hardest of hearts melt when they see her. Having a girl after three sons has been as exciting as it has been mystifying and at times frustrating. Girls are certainly more dramatic, more emotional, and more in tune with every little thing going on in a family. Ella knows where everything is and my sons could never find a thing. She loves watching me put on makeup and is already quite proficient at putting play makeup on her own face. One day she told me that I wear jeans too much and she wished I would wear dresses more often. I took her advice.

Some days Ella behaves so much like me I am convinced that nurture is stronger than nature. But then Ella does something that is so uniquely Ella and I know that nature is pulsing strongly through her veins. I have no need to have a daughter that looks like me or is "just like me," so I take pleasure in watching this unique and bright little lady grow up.

I never realized that adoption would touch our lives in so many ways. Not only do we have a daughter we adore, but our world has broadened substantially. I have met so many wonderful people and their amazing children who have also been touched by adoption. I realized that when I adopted Ella, I adopted her country of birth as well. Guatemala is now on my radar at all times. Ella and I went back for a visit in 2010 with a group of people from our community and visited an orphanage and a school. She loved visiting Guatemala and rejoiced in finding people that "looked like her," as she said.

One day while reading Ella's adoption papers, I decided that I wanted to try to find her birth mother. She was so young when she placed Ella for adoption that I could not believe she did not want future contact with us, as she had indicated in the paperwork. We found her quickly and she was elated that we had made contact.

When Ella is ready, she will go to meet her birth mother. Meanwhile, we enjoy sending photos and sharing information.

Some days I still feel like this is all a wonderful dream. This amazing little five-year-old is running around calling me "Mommy." I know that I am incredibly fortunate and that this new life is indeed good!

LINDA SKAHILL

Linda and James Skahill live in New Jersey and the U.S. Virgin Islands with their two children and five dogs.

Our two adoptions were completely different and full of totally unique emotions and issues. Our daughter was adopted from Armenia. It was a parent-initiated independent adoption. We did not use an adoption agency and did everything ourselves, and it was very difficult to navigate. Once we managed to get through all the government red tape, we came home with a perfectly healthy eleven-month-old baby girl. We knew nothing about her parental background. I was happy not knowing anything about the birth mother/family because I didn't want to live with the threat of anyone changing his/her mind about the adoption. I didn't want my child to have memories of her previous family and I didn't want my daughter wanting her birth mother instead of me. I have a daughter who only once in a while wishes she knew what her "belly mama" looked like, as she grapples with finding herself while growing into a lovely girl.

Our second adoption was a five-year-old boy from Ethiopia. It was so much easier and less stressful to have a great adoption agency doing everything for us. When we got to Addis to pick him up, we had the opportunity to meet with his birth family. We found a meeting place, but the birth family had to walk for an hour or more to get to us. They walked because they didn't have a car and because there weren't many roads. No car and no roads were alien thoughts for me. Real poverty is something I had not experienced. I think it exists for me as some kind of fantasy and even with photos in magazines, you can't really know what it means. When you see it firsthand, though, it is life changing. In the town where my son's family lived, I saw plenty of poverty and starvation, and it was shocking.

I met my son's birth mother, one of his brothers, and one of his sisters. That was the most intense moment of my life. I looked into the eyes of a woman who was my age, and she was giving up her youngest child to me. I felt an enormous weight. Here I was, the luckiest person in the world with everything anyone would want. I have a great family, a successful business, a beautiful home, so many opportunities, and I started to imagine what this woman was thinking. I thought that she was making such a brave decision. Was she hoping it was right? Was she hoping her son would some-day understand and not hate her? She was probably hoping that he would have a better life with me than in Ethiopia.

We had an interpreter and we spoke about what we wanted for "our son" who was "her son," and I promised her that I would take care of him and then we hugged and cried. I took photos of her with her family and we all posed together for a photo. I framed them and put them in his room. I feel compelled to send her updates and photos. I even copy his report card for her. It's funny that I hated the thought of all of this nine years ago with my daughter. The thought of having to check in and the feeling of being judged are gone. Now that I have my son and I know his mother, I feel happy to reassure her. In fact, I can't wait to send her the next report. I want her to see how well he's doing. I want her to know he's okay.

My son, as much as he misses his birth family, is old enough to understand that he has better opportunities living with us. He has gone through his grief process, but he misses his Ethiopian family from time to time. My daughter now sees both sides of adoption. She sees her brother, who knows his birth mother and adoptive mother and has occasional grief. She knows herself as the adopted child who knows only her adoptive mother and who grieves for her birth mother. We all talk about it openly and privately with each child. We meet grown adopted children and newly adopted children all the time. My children know that adoption is normal and not a taboo subject, so they feel at ease discussing it. They ask great questions. I'm impressed with their resilience and ability to be flexible in all situations.

While the adoption road is fraught with scary moments, it's the greatest road to travel. The fear of your children not loving you, or you not loving them, is the real fear. We loved our children the moment we saw them, and now we have two children that love us unconditionally.

It took my son, who is not a huggy or kissy kid, one year and four months to finally hug me, and he smooched my cheek and said, "I love you, Mom." That washed every bit of the trauma, heartache, and difficulty away forever.

The Skahill kids

FRANK

Frank lives in New York City with his son, Peter, who was
adopted from China.

I was very lucky. When I was a kid, I had two great parents. Growing up, I always used to think how much better a world it would be
if everyone had great parents. And it's always been heartbreaking
for me to think of a child without any parents at all. So I've always
wanted to adopt, whether I was married or not.

I chose to adopt from China because, after spending some
time teaching Chinese toddlers in China, when I imagined myself
with children, the children were always Chinese! So it just seemed
natural.

The process was long and uncertain for me as a single man, but
three agencies and two prospective children later, it finally came
through, just months before the Chinese government banned all
single-parent adoptions. I decided on a waiting child, and in some
ways left it up to fate to choose the one for me. How do you choose
a child from a catalog anyway? The agency suggested they send me
the full dossiers on the latest three toddler boys, and I agreed. I
had a feeling my future son was one of these three, and he was. I
still remember the last words of his dossier, roughly translated as,
"He steals *you* heart."

He certainly had my heart by the time I arrived in China. Ms.
Zhang was one of the orphanage officials who brought my son to
the provincial capital to finalize the adoption. As we bid farewell
on the last day, Ms. Zhang simply broke down. It was so terribly

sad. I'll never forget it. We're still in touch, though, and I plan to bring my son back next year to visit her and his first home.

Peter adapted seamlessly. As long as he could play, he was fine. He loved to eat too, though that was one area that needed some work. It took a while to wean him off what I imagine was a very strict time limit for meals at the orphanage. *"Kuai chi!"* he would repeat over and over ("Eat quickly!"), while grabbing every bit of food on the table. His hands, mouth, and cheeks were stuffed full, and his eyes were wide as he scanned the table for whatever he could grab next.

Peter used to stare at my knees, extend his arms like a bird, and patiently wait for the big liftoff. He loved being held and carried by his new dad, even on day one. It's been a miracle watching him grow. When I remember to break from my endless chores, I sit back and just watch him. It still fascinates me that he's here and that we're together from opposite sides of the earth, my love and my life.

LYNN DANZKER

Lynn is an entrepreneur who runs an executive recruiting firm and a business in the renewable energy sector. She resides in northern New Jersey with her husband, Joe, a talented photographer, and her beautiful adopted son.

I dreamed of being a mom as far back as I can remember. Yet as my forty-second birthday approached, I found myself single, childless, with no prospects for marriage, *and* distraught. With all of my success, the ache in my heart to be a mom just wouldn't go away. I grew up in a traditional family with a dad who worked and a mom who stayed at home to raise my brother and me. We lived in a modest home with a white picket fence and we had a dog. That was my definition of family *and* the only one I could imagine for myself.

After a great deal of soul searching and with the support of three extraordinary friends, I embarked on the journey of single motherhood.

Plan A: In vitro fertilization—after all, I wanted my baby to have *at least* part of my DNA. I soon learned that I had a 1 percent chance of conceiving, with an equally low percentage of having a healthy baby. Taking this journey alone was just *too* risky.

Plan B: Adoption was something I would never, *ever* have considered in the past! I had heard too many domestic adoption stories in which the birth mother changed her mind.

I chose international adoption where the birth parents were unknown. This plan offered a guarantee that I would get a very young baby. I chose Russia because I have Russian ancestry, they allow single women to adopt (not all countries do), and I could choose the gender.

The process for an international adoption is *daunting*. I was given a fourteen-page application questioning everything about my family, my childhood, how I will support and raise the child, who will be the male role model, how I will care for the child, and more. I had to provide documents proving my citizenship, income, and place of residence; letters from employers, accountants, and doctors; FBI background checks and references from friends and family, *and on and on*. There were interviews with a social worker who was assigned to my case and a list of seminars I had to attend. Medical exams, psychological tests, and of course lots of money were required to complete the adoption.

I chose an international adoption agency that had ten years of experience with Russian adoptions and had worked with single women. When the application arrived, I decided to spend a long weekend at my vacation home in Vermont to complete it. I would need a clear head, I thought. The next day I woke up to a picture-perfect ski day in Vermont and decided to go skiing for a few hours; the application would have to wait until later. That morning a handsome, kind, single man asked if I would join him on the chair-lift. Who would have known that invitation would change the course of my life?

Joe and I were engaged ten months later on the top of that very mountain in Vermont. We brought our twenty-one-month-old son, Cole, home from Russia eight months later. Cole is now four and a half years old, and Joe and I just celebrated our second wedding anniversary.

So how do I define a family? In my case, neither the definition nor the journey was what I had imagined, but the experience and the love the three of us share are more than I could have ever hoped for.

"Three paths, two continents, one love—three hearts now beat as one . . ."

—Written by Lynn and Joe for Cole's adoption announcement

Lynn Danzker and Joe Epstein with their son,
Cole Danzker Epstein

ANDREW VAUGHAN

Andrew is a psychologist in New York, where he lives with his wife, Lisa, and five children, Jack, Brittany, Emily, Sam, and Max.

Meet Jack. When Jack was a couple of months old, his birth parents in China placed him in a hotel room. That was brave. I suppose they chose a hotel room because they wanted him to be safe and found. They didn't want him to be alone for too long. He wasn't. We adopted Jack when he was nine months old. He was a floppy little creature and we loved him right away.

Jack was alert and very much a thinker right from the start. When he was four years old, we were in our hotel room at Disneyland, and out of the blue he matter-of-factly blurted out, "Is this the hotel where they found me?" It was on his mind.

In 2003 at the time of year when the anniversary memorials of September 11 were being televised nonstop, we were all sitting together. Jack proudly stated with all the certainty you can imagine, "My birth father is a fireman." It was on his mind.

We always told Jack that he came from God, then spent some time with his birth parents, then spent some time at the Shanghai Children's Welfare Institute, and then came home to us. One day, when Jack was five, out of left field he asked me, "So where did God come from?" It was on his mind.

I am a history buff, and one day I was watching a documentary on Tiananmen Square. Jack came bopping into the room and he was intrigued. We had a very nice discussion about freedom of speech and different systems of government. A few weeks later we were at the dinner table and Jack burst into tears. We hugged him and when he finally calmed down he explained that he was sad because he didn't want his birth parents to be in jail from Tiananmen Square. It was on his mind.

Jack is a sensitive soul. Grandma Theresa gave him a present. It was a nice rugby shirt, deep maroon and navy blue, with a fancy crest on it. He refused to wear it for some reason. I pressed Jack by telling him, "Wear it. It's nice. It looks like a shirt Harry Potter would wear." He still refused. I pressed him more, trying to guilt him into wearing it with a moralistic lecture on appreciation. Jack became upset and told me, "I would wear it if I had round eyes like Emily." It was on his mind.

Emily is one of Jack's sisters. She's from Russia. Emily came home to us after a detour. That detour was a "disrupted adoption." This is an unfortunate phrase that turned out to be a fortunate process for us and Emily. She was born in a Moscow hospital to a birth mother who gave a false name and a false address and then left the hospital. I think her mother was brave, because she knew that she didn't have the capacity to raise the baby, yet she still wanted the baby to be delivered safely, be cared for, and not be alone for too long.

The hospital staff named the baby Vera, and Vera remained in that Moscow hospital for six weeks. No visitors came, so she was taken to Baby Home 23, an orphanage where she remained until she was two years old. She was adopted and brought to the United States by a kind and good family who also soon made a brave decision. They realized they did not have the capacity to raise her. I'm a psychologist and I had evaluated her for developmental delays. A couple of days later I received a call from the child's adoption social worker who asked if I knew of any family who would be interested in readopting this little girl. We immediately said that we wanted her. Four days later she came home to us and she became our little Emily Vera. The social worker involved in Emily's adoption was the same social worker we used for Jack's adoption years earlier. It really is a small world.

About a month later we went to a neighbor's party, where a particularly curious and insensitive guest repeatedly asked obnoxious questions right in front of our children, "Is she *yours*? Is he *yours*?" You get the idea. The party dragged on. Jack started to misbehave. I figured he was tired and it was time to go home. When I was tucking him in bed that night, I reminded Jack how it's very important to behave nicely at parties. Jack looked me in the eyes and firmly asked, "Are you going to give me away?" It was on his mind.

Two years later we were waiting to adopt a baby from South Korea. There was some paperwork trouble and we weren't sure if we would be approved. We waited and waited. The adoption agency told us we could expect our referral "in one week," and Jack said, "I spoke to God and the baby will come home on Tuesday." Tuesday came and went. One week turned to two, then three, then four, then five. I worried, but the world kept going. As a die-hard pessimist, I started losing hope. Then we got the call that our baby from God via South Korea would arrive home on August 29, which was a Tuesday.

Recently, we were invited to an event celebrating adoption. We all dressed up and we played hooky from work and school and drove a couple of hours to get there. A hundred kids from all over the world were there. The kids in our family formed their own little U.N. delegation, with Jack and Max from China, Brittany from the United States, Emily from Russia, and Sam from South Korea.

The day was sunny, wonderful, exhilarating, and exhausting. It was time to go home. As my wife, Lisa, buckled the kids into their car seats, she said, "You guys are awesome!" And Jack blurted out, "We're awesome because of you."

So I'm writing this essay now to tell my children to never forget that Mommy and I are awesome because of you. We love you so much, forever, no matter what.

Vaughan siblings

CINDY SUTLIFF

*Cindy Sutliff works for the New York eHealth Collaborative on
statewide policy guidance for health information exchange.
She and her husband, Cal Sutliff, live in Brooklyn, New York.
Their daughter, Huong Sutliff, who was adopted from Vietnam
at age six, now attends Bates College in Maine.*

The day finally arrived. Cal and I and our adoption agency liaison
traveled by van to the Hoa Binh orphanage, where we were scheduled to pick up our daughter. The morning was thick with mist as
we drove for what seemed like hours through the glorious, lush
countryside of Vietnam. Bicycles and motor scooters dodged everywhere. As we drove deeper into the mountains, the quiet surrounded our van. We could only imagine what was in store for us.

The Giving and Receiving Ceremony was a symbolic event yet
moving and very emotional. Tears streamed down the faces of the
caretakers who had gotten to know our daughter, Huong, and down
our faces as we welcomed her into our lives. Huong was six years old
and full of energy and curiosity. She was beautiful, but there was a
sadness about her that day. I can only imagine how frightening it
must have been to see these two strangers and be told they were
now her new mommy and daddy. She was old enough to remember
so much about her life with her village family and her life in the
orphanage. She did not speak English. We did not speak Vietnamese. How was this all going to work? How could we possibly help
her through the transition and make her feel safe? She was about to
face so many new things: first ride in a car; first time in a hotel; first

time on an airplane; first time in a city with cars honking, strange people, tall buildings, big houses. All of this was unimaginable.

We arrived at Kennedy International Airport and our dear friend Amy was there to greet us. She welcomed us and helped transport us to our home in Brooklyn, where we were welcomed by our son, Tai. The adventure began. I took maternity leave for four months. Huong was small, frightened, yet eager. We spent nights trying to comfort her when she woke up screaming. I would spend hours sleeping beside her restless little body. Finally, we decided to create a family bed. That seemed to work. Huong and I spent the days singing songs to each other. Hers were in Vietnamese and mine in English. We visited the playground and we walked through the park and the neighborhood. We went to the dentist and we visited Dr. Jane and got all of her parasites cleared up. We danced, we dressed up, we drew pictures and told stories about the pictures. We laughed and we cried. It was a time of wonder and a time of adjustment for everyone.

Slowly the words and recognition of objects became apparent and Huong could finally communicate in English. I think that helped her settle down a bit. She began to feel safe. We were not going away and we were not sending her away. She began to trust us. That felt good. We hugged a lot, read stories, and watched TV together. Huong had always been in an environment with lots of children and now she was with two grown-ups all the time with few exceptions. We enrolled her in a ballet program thinking that she did not need language to follow along. She was strong, graceful, and athletic. We knew she could do it and she did. It was a wonderful way for her to begin to experience the social side of life again. She loved to dance and we loved watching her as she grew into her new life within our family.

There were so many firsts with Huong: first snowfall, first full sentence in English, first night sleeping alone in her own bed, first day at school, first day ice-skating, first friends, first Christmas, and first birthday party.

Keeping much of her Vietnamese heritage intact was important to us and we think important to Huong as she grew into this new American culture. We celebrated all of the Vietnamese special holidays such as the Moon Festival in the fall and Tet, Vietnamese New Year, in the winter. We dressed in traditional Vietnamese costume for these occasions, ate traditional Vietnamese food, and shared memories of Vietnam while looking at photos from our trip. Huong wrote stories about her past life and family in Vietnam. She drew pictures of everything and we talked about what the pictures meant to her.

Huong was home. She settled in and she opened herself up to loving and trusting us and letting us love her back. She was like a sponge soaking up all of the learning. She continues to challenge herself and is wise beyond her years. She is strong, resilient, loving, and kind. Huong will be a junior at Bates College in the fall and will be studying art history in Florence, Italy, as part of her semester abroad program. We are so very proud of her many accomplishments. She inspires us and has been a joyous gift in our lives.

KRISTINE NESSLAR

Kristine and her husband, Yancey, live in Illinois with their sons Quinn and Belaye.

Dear Dr. Aronson:

It has been four months since Belaye has come home to us and I thought you would like to know how well he is doing. When Belaye came into care in Ethiopia, last June, he weighed 18–19 pounds. In the nine months that he was in care, he remained the same weight. I was concerned about what that meant for him once he was home. I'm thrilled to write that in the four months he has been home he has gained almost five pounds! He's also an inch or two taller; it is a bit difficult to get him to stay still and stand tall against the wall while I take a pencil and mark his progress, but we can tell from the length of his pants, if nothing else, that he is getting taller. He has outgrown his first set of shoes and his pants are now mostly staying up because he has a bit of a tush finally!

His language has exploded! He repeats everything Quinn, his brother, says and that has helped him reach an astounding level of proficiency in English. Every night at dinner Quinn tells us in his typically very animated way about his day at school and as he is talking, Belaye is right there with him, repeating every word as best he can.

His first favorite phrase is "Wha's appening?" It is used for everything from the milk spilling in the morning, to seeing *one of us put on our shoes to go outside. His second favorite phrase learned from Quinn, no doubt, is "Wha chew doin'?" This is usually said when one of us comes in to find he is doing something he shouldn't be doing. When I walk into the bathroom to find he is playing in the sink and the water is on and overflowing onto the floor, I will hear "Wha chew doin'?!" as I turn off the water. It never fails to make me smile even if it usually means I'm cleaning up something or other.*

Needless to say, everyone who meets him is charmed. This is not to say that he doesn't behave like a typical three-year-old, because he does; he also has major grief and insecurity issues from all that he has been through in Ethiopia. However, he is beginning to let us comfort him at night and he sometimes relaxes enough to actually be quiet. He is slowly blossoming into who he is as a person.

I don't think I ever told you how close we came to not accepting his referral. Having given birth to a baby who was born 9 pounds 6 ounces, I just couldn't get my mind around what 19 pounds meant for a three-year-old. I wanted to make sure we were not committing to more than we were capable of, especially as Yancey and I both work. If it were not for you and our confidence in your experience we very well might have said no. I am teary-eyed thinking of the loss to our family if we had not adopted Belaye.

Thank you for all your kindness and hard work. My Aunt Sylvia used to tell me that angels were the prayers of others sent to watch over us. You are surrounded by angels as we think of you every day and wish you well on your mission.

I sent you a Facebook invitation should you ever wish to see video of Belaye and Quinn.

No need to respond. Just wanted to let you know how well Belaye is doing in our family. He is a joy.

Hope your family is well and your summer is going swimmingly.

Kindest regards,
Kristine Nesslar

VI.

A New Life

*I knew that he spoke not a word of English and that we spoke
only three words in his native tongue. What I did not know was
that our real differences were deeper and more mysterious.*
—Claude Knobler

C hildren who travel worlds to finally find their place within a
permanent family experience a complicated mixture of
emotions—from excitement and relief to feelings of loss for what
they have left behind, if only because it was familiar. In the essays
that follow, parents share how their children adapted to life in
America. Even everyday adaptations like learning to use stairs, toi-
lets, or electric lights can be profound. Many children arrive from
their poor birth countries where food is scarce and are overwhelmed by the abundance of food now available to them; they
think they should eat everything in front of them in case it suddenly disappears. One compassionate father notes: "Who could
forget her automatic response to almost everything? An emphatic
'no' likely was what kept her sane. We learned and she learned."

I recently visited with a friend who has three adopted children from Guatemala, and we shared memories of the weeks and months following our children's arrival. We both felt that these were some of the most exciting yet exhausting times in the journey to create our families. My son Des used to fall asleep at dinner from the fatigue of trying to understand English while he was still thinking in Amharic (his Ethiopian language). Making a new home really *home* is a long, circuitous, and unpredictable process that eventually results in peace and balance for most children who are adopted.

The nonadopted new siblings of these adopted children are often the most capable of sweetly charting the progress of their adopted sibling's assimilation. This is beautifully expressed by the older sister of a brother adopted from Ethiopia, whose full story begins on page 234. She writes, "It took me a while to figure out why they were looking at us. I would forget that our family was different than other families. I would forget sometimes that Nati's skin was a different color, that his eyes were brown and not blue, and that his hair was black and not blond. One day, one of my friend's parents came up to me and said, 'Wow Grace, you look so much like your brother!' I replied, 'Which one?' Nati fit into our family perfectly."

THERESA REBECK

Theresa Rebeck is a playwright and novelist and created
Smash *for television. She lives in Brooklyn, New York, with her*
husband, Jess Lynn, and their children, Cooper and Cleo.

Our excellent daughter, Cleo Juan Rebeck Lynn, was born in Anhui Province in or around the city of Hefei, in November of 2001.
When she was one day old, her biological parents took her to the
gate of the local orphanage, the Hefei Children's Welfare Institute,
and left her there in the dead of night. In their love and their terror, it was the absolute safest place they could imagine. And they
were right. The institute took her in and named her Zhang Dong
Juan, which means pretty winter girl, for she was found in the
middle of winter and even at one day old it was apparent this little girl was going to be a looker.

For fourteen months Zhang Dong Juan was cared for by the
amazing women who worked in the institute, and when we came
to get her she was a happy and healthy little person with a touch of
bronchitis. She could walk and say a few words in Mandarin. She
could pick up a Cheerio with two fingers. She loved to play, and
could sit quietly for hours putting little cups inside each other and
then taking them apart again. When we got back to Brooklyn, she
fell in love with our dog immediately, and would follow her around
the house, pulling her tail.

This summer Cleo is ten. She is a wonderful artist and a great
joker. Her quite striking good looks are accentuated by a purple
streak she insists on putting in her hair. She likes to play with little

things and builds huge, complex dioramas on the floor of her bedroom out of Legos, Playmobil sets, and Littlest Pet Shop critters. And she loves animals—dogs, cats, rabbits, horses. When we go to Vermont in the summer, we sign her up for the local two-week horse camp.

Unfortunately, this year no one else signed up for the first week of camp, so the nice people at Mountain View Ranch decided that Cleo could come and take some lessons and do some trail rides and just hang out with the horses and the girls who take care of them. This sounded like a fine idea to us, so we took them up on their offer.

The first day we showed up there was in fact one other little girl there. Her parents were visiting from Italy, where the father worked as a sculptor. They had come to this part of Vermont because there's a good marble quarry here. And their daughter had somehow, the day before, found a flyer for this horse camp.

Their daughter, Michelle, was clearly adopted from China, as it turned out.

She was born in Hefei, Anhui Province. She had been raised at the Hefei Children's Welfare Institute. And yes, she was also ten years old. As we stood on a remote mountainside in Danby, Vermont, we realized that the girls had been at the same orphanage, halfway around the world, at the same time, ten years ago. They may well have been roommates.

This discovery was met by the two girls with something resembling utter indifference. Cleo and Michelle would run off to the stables while we parents found out what we could about all the lives that had so spectacularly collided on this remote mountainside. Her father, Giancarlo, was a sculptor, and her mother, Germana, an editor. They traveled with Giancarlo's sculpting partner,

Jill. Jill and Giancarlo mostly sculpted monuments like angels, tombstones, madonnas. They spent much of their year in Italy, when they weren't in the United States. We were enchanted by the international panache of their stories. They were impressed with my less magical Broadway adventures. (Giancarlo termed them "scary.")

We had a great two weeks. The girls would finish camp, go get milk shakes, fall asleep in the car, and then go swimming. The parents would consider them, and one another, with wonder. "You might understand it, if we had met in Manhattan," Jill observed. "But this really is the middle of nowhere." It *was* the middle of nowhere, and there was no one else there except a couple of Italian sculptors, an Italian editor, an American playwright, an American father, and two girls from China. And there on the hillside under a brilliant sky, Giancarlo burst into tears as we watched those two

Cleo Rebeck Lynn on horseback in Vermont

tiny girls, children of China and children of the world and children of five parents who loved them, make their horses mind them.

The Icelandic sagas tell us that while Rome was ruling the Mediterranean, before America was discovered, before England was civilized, the tribes of the northern seas would adopt each other's children. It was their way of binding themselves to one other, of making the world one tribe and one people. I know this ancient wisdom because I live it every day.

MEGHAN GILBERT-HICKEY

Meghan Gilbert-Hickey, a writer and teacher, lives in New York City with her amazing husband, her two breathtaking biological daughters, and her heart-melting, complicatedly perfect adopted son.

He is Mine and Not Mine.

Of course, that's the most we can say of any of our children, biological or adopted, if we are honest with ourselves, which we are often not. Before Dylan came home with us from Seoul, he belonged to his birth mother and father for the first few days of his life, a nurse, and two foster mothers. He belongs to them still, and although he doesn't know it now, he always will.

And yet, they've lost him, for the time being, at least. They've lost the ability to watch him grow, to hear him laugh, to feel him cry. I saw it happen, with the last foster mother. I saw her eyes melt, even as her face hardened into a good-bye smile. I watched her watch him become someone else's son, and I felt her claim on him as if it were a tangible thing. I carry her loss with me as a reminder of the enormity of my gain.

These losses are felt in the same way I feel his weight sinking into my hip and his burrowing into my collarbone. I carry his losses most of all: the man he might have been but will not be, and his birth mother who had to say that first good-bye. I carry her losses: the son she does not know, the smile, always open-mouthed and close-eyed that she does not see, and the deep-breathing sleep she cannot watch with awe.

My connection to the birth mother is a challenge. I too am a birth mother. I have carried two daughters in my womb, but I did not and do not have to share them with another mother. I have not experienced her bittersweet loss. I am trying to understand how she might feel right now. I think that she is sharing Dylan with me, because I feel that I am learning to share him with her.

I am a new mother once again, because I am Dylan's new mother. Learning to be his mother feels very, very new. At night, as I snuggle him off to sleep, my breathing slows to match his sweet breaths and I think about those other mothers. I think about their frustrations, their joys, and how much they, inevitably, miss him now. I push past my own exhaustion to remain mindful of the privilege of his trust and to treasure the gift of watching his eyes flutter shut.

I promise I'll be his last mother, the one he gets to keep. My hope is for him to keep all of them, just as they will keep him. And until the day that he can seek them out on his own, I will carry them for him, just as I carry him every night to bed.

Meghan Gilbert-Hickey's three children

JILL VEXLER

Jill holds a Ph.D. in anthropology and specializes in curating museum exhibitions about world cultures and social history. She and her daughter live in New York City and travel as often as they can to Texas, Mexico, and other parts of the world.

Off the plane from Ethiopia, the ultra-gregarious Tibarek took to Washington Square like an old politician who is campaign stumping. She disappeared on the spiral slide, only to emerge with a giggling baby between her legs. The baby's parents were thrilled that a "big girl" was taking care of their daughter, comfortably commenting that she clearly knew how to handle little ones. Moments later, surrounded by a group of American kids, mostly bigger than she, Tibarek was speaking animatedly (in what language?) as all heads nodded as if following orders for the next game. I hadn't needed Amharic back in Addis Ababa to know that this five-and-a-half-year-old was social, talkative, funny, and smart. My friends in Addis were amazed and amused with her clever and grown-up Amharic. I longed to catch the nuances that were clearly lost in translation. She would often end her declarations, they told me, with the phrase "You know," which led to great laughter. Months later, when "You know" entered her English style of speaking, I felt a core piece of her had emerged just as that nonverbal leadership and self-assuredness had on the playground her first day.

At public school, her English soared, as did her friendships. On the first day of second grade, when Tibarek saw the principal and vice principal in a receiving line, she joined right in, shaking hands with dozens of parents and children who entered. The seasoned ESL (English as a Second Language) teacher told me that during her career, no child had ever learned English as well or as quickly as Tibarek. How did she gauge this? Through Tibarek's inflection and ability to use a new word in another context, she practiced her new language, English. Oddly enough, her kindergarten teacher never once commented on her language skills, even though she walked in barely knowing a word of English. Neither did that same teacher in first grade when her English sounded fluent. In second and third, when teachers criticized her writing as "not grade level," they didn't take into consideration that for almost six years of her life, until two and three years before, there was another language that was her mother tongue.

One teacher told me that it would have been "intrusive" to have looked at her dossier to find out that she wasn't American by birth. "I thought she was just . . ." I bit my tongue. I was never worried about her writing. I'm more worried about those shallow teachers who judged her without knowing her, who thought that being social was a negative, and who implied that she had too many privileges, like an American Girl doll, and who said in front of Tibarek that a nine-year-old African girl should be able to do her hair by herself. Insanity. Would that teacher please talk to African or African American women about their hair and who does it? Everyone has a helper!

Today, however, I write about the same little girl, now age ten, still kind to little ones, smart, super-social, defending her friends from prejudicial comments, generous, and funny, yet with a young woman's body, menarche and puberty in full motion. As I think about the changes that menarche brings, I'm reminded of my adoption counselor's words: raising an adopted child is like raising *any* child but more so! There is simply an added level of complexity and more unknowns than with a biological child. Tibarek is entering this phase when I've had only four years of mothering of this little girl. I thought I'd have until twelve. Please? But no, this is who she is. And as the recent statistical analysis reveals, adopted children (and I would posit, especially those adopted at an older age) enter puberty some eighteen months before the U.S. average.

She's still a little girl who giggles and dives under the pillows when Prince William and Kate kiss, and has her impish, trickster moments, and loves *High School Musical* and Selena Gomez. She seems to have skipped "tween" and gone straight to "teen." She may still love Barney and have a moment of SpongeBob (in secret), but the movie *Prom* weighs in heavily. The mixture is kind of wonderful, and loving her with new complexity is part of my growth too. The mistakes they make, like the first lie, even have a little humor, but the teen stuff is really hard if not terrifying. "I don't care!" spoken with a new defiance, the walls put up, and oppositional behavior to the nth degree are very hard for me.

I am sorting through the reality that I didn't get enough time with Tibarek as a little girl. I try to adjust to her need to disappear while we walk down the street and let her walk to school alone occasionally (as I hold my breath!). I also try to empathize with what must be her own amazement and probable bewilderment with her new body. The good part is that she isn't hiding her development and has divine African posture. When another little girl adopted from Ethiopia asked her if she was the tallest and oldest girl in her class, she responded, "Yes." When the other girl replied that she was too and didn't like it, Tibarek said, "Well, why don't you think it's cool to be what you are?" I almost dropped my jaw with her insight and maturity (and my pride!). So, something is in order. But when her period started, big changes were wrought and tough times began.

All menarche has its difficulties and early menarche even more so. Suddenly, after forty years as an anthropologist, I finally realize that a "menstrual hut" isn't sexist. Au contraire, it's a societal and architectural solution to the privacy needed and emotions expressed during menstruation. If only a menstrual hut could fit in our New York loft! I needed help with this one, just as I did with crying jags or immunizations. I checked with my shrink friends and with mothers who have been through this "phase." I keep digging deeper into myself. Why is this so hard if it's "normal"? If individuation is so important, as I firmly believe, why is this chapter in her individuation so painful? We're still attaching and it's time to individuate already?

I return to adoption. Perhaps these changes are exacerbated by an extra degree of pushing limits and buttons to test me to make sure she is really here to stay. Perhaps she is angry with me, with her biological mother, and with all sorts of things hard to pinpoint. Perhaps it is yet another level of attachment, another questioning of why she is part of *this* family and not *that* one. Maybe she is asking why she isn't in Ethiopia and why she has to keep Passover and not eat pasta and tortillas? The push-pull of attachment and separation/individuation are sophisticated concepts and hard realities to accept daily.

It's all new to me. After four months of maxipads, I'm still figuring out ways not to buy into the anger and fierce independence while still structuring what she does. I'm working on accepting that things we used to do together don't work for her anymore. I'm seeing that right now we are different in ways that I wish we weren't. I know that this will change. Expressions of love and affection, which

have always been hard for her, are diminished, and my sweet ges-
tures toward her are met with a scrunched-up face.

I'm finding that old adages take on new meanings. I've always
liked the one about giving our children wings so they can fly. At
this moment, it's way too early for her to fly solo. Among my challenges is finding the way to guide her flight path during this growth
spurt without clipping her wings.

Tibarek and her mother, Jill Vexler

CAL SUTLIFF

*Cal and Cindy Sutliff live in Brooklyn, New York. Cal works as
a management consultant throughout the United States
and Canada, and Cindy works for the New York eHealth
Collaborative on statewide policy guidance for health
information exchange. Their daughter, Huong, now attends
Bates College.*

Back in 1997, Huong was living with her parents and five siblings
in a village in the mountains of northern Vietnam. She was number
four in the birth order, and at six years old, was the one assigned to stay home and take care of her two younger siblings
while the rest of the family labored in the rice paddies. Cooking
and child care for two young children is a tough assignment for a
six-year-old.

Later when the parents with "too many mouths to feed" decided to put Huong up for international adoption, she began her
four-month-long stay in an orphanage in Hoa Binh. Her memory
of those four months when she visited it ten years later was "I remember this as a happy place, and I had enough to eat for the first
time."

The story of Cindy and I, her new parents, meeting Huong for
the first time and her feelings as she left the orphanage for the long
trip to Brooklyn were captured beautifully five years later when, at
eleven, she wrote a piece that was eventually published in the *New
York Times*.

I have many early memories of Huong. Within hours of arrival in our home, she was going through every room in the house, exploring each closet, opening every drawer and examining its contents before moving on to the next treasure site. I also remember the tears streaming down her face the one and only time I placed her in time-out. Who could forget her automatic response to almost everything? An emphatic "no" likely was what kept her sane. We learned and she learned.

I remember returning from food shopping with her, and in the unpacking process, I was shocked to see a forty-pound bag of dog food walking toward me as it almost completely blocked out the hardworking little girl carrying it. She couldn't have weighed more than sixty pounds herself at that point. I also remember years later, when as a teenager, nothing could convince her to pick up a heavy bag of any kind!

She never lost her ability to work hard, however, transferring it instead to her studies. Math was a particular nemesis. Math tutoring and special math classes seemed endless. But she wouldn't give up. As I write this, we just learned yesterday that she has completed her math requirement as a sophomore at Bates College with a final, glorious B-. This was her lowest spring semester grade but probably her most significant success. What an amazing fourteen years this has been.

GRACE KNOBLER

Grace Knobler is the sister of Nati Knobler, who was adopted from Ethiopia, and lives in Los Angeles with her parents, two brothers, a dog, cat, and fish. She is currently hoping to get one more dog and then in a few years go to college with it.

When I was five, my parents came to my older brother and me and asked, "Do you want to adopt a child from Ethiopia?" I immediately responded, *"Yes!"* My older brother, who was seven at the time, took longer to answer. He was wiser and knew what adopting a kid would mean for his life in the future. After a few days of thought, he came to the same conclusion that I had. All I thought about was having a younger brother, someone I could love and hang out with, and a new member of the Knobler family. I had made a decision in thirty seconds that would permanently change my life.

After my family watched adoption videos and finished the paperwork, we sent care packages to my new brother, Nati. The care packages included toys, stickers, and photo albums. Later we received a photo of him, a little boy with big cheeks, soon to become my younger brother. I brought this picture to my kindergarten class, along with the new snow globe I had just gotten. When it was my turn, I stood up and presented the picture, proudly claiming, "This is my new brother and he is from Ethiopia; his name is Nati and this is my new snow globe." The news of my new brother came as a surprise to all of the parents in the room. I went on to present the snow globe because at the time I didn't really think the news of the adoption was a big deal. It seemed so natural to me. Of course I was excited, but the reason I only took thirty seconds to answer "the big question" was because I didn't see what the big deal was. All of my friends had younger brothers. I saw all the people's shocked faces around me as I announced the news. At the age of five I had no idea what I was getting myself into.

When Nati first came, families would give us strange looks. It took me a while to figure out why they were looking at us. I would forget that our family was different than other families. I would forget sometimes that Nati's skin was a different color, that his eyes were brown and not blue, and that his hair was black and not blond. One day, one of my friend's parents came up to me and said, "Wow Grace, you look so much like your brother!" I replied, "Which one?" Nati fit into our family perfectly.

Nati is not an ordinary child; we knew that when we watched the adoption video. He was addicted to the camera, always making faces at it. As soon as the camera attempted to move to a different area, Nati would follow it and be right back on the screen. He was very energetic. We knew he would be perfect for our family, and that turned out to be true. Even though his energy causes many arguments, Nati couldn't be better for the Knobler family. His excitement makes the members of my family laugh and smile. Because of his energy, we fight. He likes to cause arguments over little things, but these arguments end quickly and he has us laughing again.

I made a decision in thirty seconds that would change my life forever. Thirty seconds is not very long to decide you want a new brother, but I know even if I had taken weeks to come to a conclusion, I would have said yes. I do not regret my decision. Yes, sometimes Nati and I scream at each other, but we also share laughs and hugs. Even though he was not born in the same family as me, I love him as much as my biological brother, Clay. He is just as much a Knobler as my mom, Mary, my dad, Claude, my brother Clay, and me, Grace. Nati is the perfect fit for the Knobler family. When you make a decision in only thirty seconds, you are usually sure of what you want; I didn't need weeks to decide because I had always wanted a younger brother. Thirty seconds was all the time I needed.

MAUREEN HUFF

Maureen Huff works in public relations and lives in New York City with her children, Abinet and Hanna.

All parents experience some sense of wonder about becoming a parent. I do believe it's heightened with adoptive parents, who always, consciously or subconsciously, think of what might have been if they had not become parents. Living in New York City is surreal, even to most Americans, yet my children just take it all in stride. They enjoy the subways, the buildings, the noise, and the beauty of so many people. Both kids innately learned how to hail a cab within months of coming to live in New York. Seeing Hanna, at barely eleven pounds, sticking out her arm without any prompting was quite a sight. I am in awe of my two kids.

My story, now our story, owes a lot to fate. I've known for the better part of my life that I wanted to adopt children. While filling out forms for the adoption agency, there was a question in the application that asked what kind of personality I imagined/dreamed about for my prospective child. I didn't put a lot of thought into it, and ended up writing that I wanted a child with a little mischief in his or her eyes. I got exactly what I had asked for in my son, Abinet.

When I brought him home a few years ago, he was eighteen months old and he was full of energy and loved to explore. That summer was a world of wonder for the both of us. Splashing in puddles and checking out pockets provided us with hours of entertainment. All we needed for an afternoon was a soccer ball and a water bottle. The simple things in life, like picking a tomato from a friend's garden, are still utterly fascinating to him. Then there were the things that he (we) took for granted; one of Abinet's first sentences was "We go brunch Ocean Grill." This is certainly a very different life than he would have had in Ethiopia.

I am in awe of any child's fascination with the holidays; celebrating together brings so much more meaning. On Thanksgiving, the parade starts a few blocks north of us. Kids all over America dream of seeing the parade in person, and we get to saunter out our door and watch it together. At Christmastime we go to Belvedere Castle in Central Park to visit Santa. Two years ago it had started to snow when we went to visit Santa, and it felt like we were the only people in the park with the elves and Santa. Abinet asked Santa where the reindeer were and he explained that they have old friends at the Bronx Zoo, so they dropped Santa off and went to the zoo for the day. Santa explained that since the reindeer can't go on subways, he would go to them at the end of the day. And since a blizzard was coming, he brought Rudolph too, and that made Abinet very excited. He never even told Santa what he wanted for Christmas because he was so excited to hear that the reindeer were nearby. Santa brought him a sled, and I had the chance to teach him how to go down a hill, and that made Christmas perfect for both of us.

I had always wanted to adopt more than one child, so not long after I brought my son home, I filled out the paperwork to adopt again. I expected to hear something in a few years, but with a surprise phone call from the adoption agency last spring, I learned about Hanna. My son and daughter are biological cousins, so I was given the opportunity to adopt her. I told Abinet about Hanna and explained the connection and that they would have been raised together in Ethiopia, and he thought it was unbelievable for about a minute. By the next day, he was back to grilling me about Derek Jeter, which was such a classic reaction.

Both my children healed and thrived in my home, and I was in awe of this miraculous process. Abinet came home with a distended belly but grew quickly. Hanna was a different story, as she became increasingly ill while in Ethiopia, and I was delayed for a critical six weeks because of the Department of Homeland Security. She was just over nine pounds at seven months. Trying to figure out how to care for her when I couldn't bring her home was definitely one of the worst times of my life. Thanks to Dr. Aronson, she was thriving within weeks of arriving in the United States. I can still barely comprehend that complete turnaround.

Hanna and Abinet adored each other from the minute they met. Abinet was so excited to meet Hanna, he just glowed. Everything he does is funny and interesting to his little sister. Abinet tries to teach Hanna to sing "Take Me Out to the Ballgame," and she tosses stuffed animals at him and laughs. Abinet was always a lousy sleeper, but it turns out he just needed a sister to share a room for comfort. Listening to them talk to each other in the morning makes me happy each day. My feelings are no different than any other parent's, but I guess I feel so appreciative and lucky to have become a parent.

My children were loved by their Ethiopian family, but they couldn't take care of them. I am in constant awe about how the lives of my children have changed. I am grateful to their Ethiopian family, my supportive family and friends, and for the love they receive daily from the amazing woman who cares for them while I am at work. Most of all, I am proud of my two strong, happy, clever, and vibrant children. I'll never tire of writing about my love for them.

JUNE INDERWIES

June M. and John R. Inderwies have been married for twenty years and are raising two sons adopted from Russia. Ross is an elementary school teacher and June is the executive director and COO of a national law firm.

Our family started the adoption journey in March 2006, and we received our referrals in April 2008.

> In our dreams always
>
> In our hearts April 9, 2008
>
> In our arms May 4, 2008
>
> In our family June 17, 2008
>
> Home forever July 4, 2008

The waiting was the hardest part, followed by the paperwork and the never-ending changes to the process. With international adoption you can count on it always changing. The rules are never the same and you can't compare your journey to others'; your family's journey is personal and unique just like your children. Looking back on the process now, we can't even imagine waiting over two years for referrals, but we can't imagine our lives without our sons and are so certain they were meant to be brothers and our children. A very wise woman from our agency said, "When the time is right and the children are ready, it will all fall into place and not before." It was very hard medicine to swallow, but we have found ourselves repeating this statement to many people over the years. We were fortunate to partner with an amazing adoption agency locally, which never once lost track of us and always made us feel like we were the only family they were guiding through this long and complicated journey. Our coordinator knew when to send an e-mail or place a call even when there was no update at all. Those e-mails and calls were the most important ones because we knew our family was not forgotten. We consider this worker at the agency part of our extended family.

As much as we read and were advised, we still wanted to control everything and we wanted everything to be done our way. I still laugh about the telephone call with our beloved Dr. Jane when I discussed that one of our sons had chicken pox several months ago. She politely and correctly told me that chicken pox was not a big concern. That moment was a revelation for us. You must surround yourself with professionals who will tell you what you need to know, not what you want to hear.

We learned that children adopted from abroad might need early intervention to help them with developmental delays from being in an orphanage, and we realized that this was critical to ensure that our children would reach their potential. We also realized that there were many negative stories about international adoption, and we worked hard to not permit ourselves to be magnets for these stories.

When we visited our children in their birthplace, Russia, we were very mindful and respectful that we were visiting a country with different values, beliefs, and customs. It always made us sad when we heard a family discuss their visits abroad and focus on the negative rather than the positive. These are stories and memories you will be talking about for many years and passing on to your children. We have wonderful memories of the warm and happy baby home that gave our boys a wonderful start in life. We are grateful for the special caregivers who loved and nourished our two sons. We see the results of that love in our children each and every day. Our children will always be Russian, and Russia is a very important part of them. Adoptive parents need to respect the culture of their children and embrace it in a way that works for their family and the kids. Celebrating a Russian tradition, holiday, food, art, or music is important.

At the end of the day, all parenting, whether through adoption or birth, is not for sissies. Parents need a healthy dose of patience, perseverance, a good sense of humor, and a support system to rely upon. We must allow our children to have a lot of fun, and we must teach them independence.

CLAUDE KNOBLER

Claude lives with his wife, Mary Knobler, their three children,
and some pets in Los Angeles.

It was a lot easier before my son learned to speak English.

My wife, Mary, and I adopted Nati from Ethiopia when he was five years old. He spoke no English and we spoke only three words of Amharic, the language of most Ethiopians. When I flew with him from the orphanage in Ethiopia back to our home in Los Angeles, he was astonished not only by the airplane but by the escalator in the airport; most everything was new to him. Here are the three words of Amharic I knew. *Shent*, which means "pee." *Baca*, which means "enough." *Ishi*, which means "it's okay." Put them in any order you like and it's still not much of a conversation.

How did we do it? How did we introduce a five-year-old boy to kindergarten, car seats, TVs, French fries, two dogs, a house, and his new brother and sister? How did we teach him English? How did we manage to communicate anything at all? It was easy.

Yes, I do remember hearing Nati demand something that sounded like "meso" from the backseat of my car. It took ten minutes to figure out he was hungry, another ten minutes to figure out he wasn't asking for a Mentos candy, and a full week before I found out that what he wanted was an Ethiopian stew he'd been missing. But that, all of it, was the easy part. We pantomimed for each other, and when all else failed we spoke English very loudly and slowly and hoped for the best, and more often than not, we got it. What was really hard came long after Nati learned English and what we probably should have always known: knowing the same words can be very different from speaking the same language.

Imagine cooking a meal. Or better yet, imagine you're my grandmother and you're cooking a meal. You've got some chicken, some matzo balls, maybe some carrots and vegetables. A stove, a pot, and an hour or two of cooking time and you've got enough chicken soup to make a nice meal. Now imagine that someone gives you a bunch of Ethiopian spices, some *berbere*, a bit of *wot kimen*, and a pound of *mitmita*, and then tells you to use all of them when you make tonight's dinner. You might, if you were a very good cook, come up with something interesting. On the other hand, you certainly wouldn't be making Grandma's chicken soup anymore.

My new family is a lot like that imaginary meal. I like to read. My wife is a sweet, funny, kind woman who would rather endure oral surgery without Novocain than brag about any of her many accomplishments. My son Clay is verbal and witty and doesn't like it when I say unkind things about anyone, including politicians and fictional characters. My daughter, Grace, loves to make art, take pictures, and watch bad reality TV in bed with her mom. And then there's Nati.

Nati, who is so confident that on his first trip from Los Angeles to San Diego, when he'd been here all of six months and was all of five years old, he told me in his broken English, "No, Dad, drive the other way. It's the other way!" Nati, who said, while talking to a hotel desk clerk in Addis Ababa, Ethiopia, "English is easy! Also, I know how to dance really well!" Of course, he said that in Amharic, since he did not yet speak a single word of English, but still, he made his point. Nati, who when he'd been here one year asked if he could build a lemonade stand near where someone was selling their house so he could get more foot traffic. To say that Nati can be loud doesn't do him justice. To say that he has charisma doesn't begin to tell the story. Put it this way: I spent the first three years Nati was here searching in vain for a dial to adjust his volume. It is, I used to think, as if somehow my family and I adopted a small, black Liza Minnelli. Nati is all singing, all dancing, all the time. All. The. Time. We had been a family that sought compromise: Nati loves arguments and winning. We had been a family that valued gentle kindness: Nati loves action, noise, and excitement. We were Woody Allen and Neil Simon and generations of borscht belt humor: Nati is pratfalls, pie-in-the-face gags, and all Three Stooges rolled into one.

I knew Nati was black and that we were white. I knew he'd been Christian and that we were Jewish (surely the chicken soup metaphor tipped you off, right?). I knew that he spoke not a word of English and that we spoke only three words in his native tongue. What I did not know was that our real differences were deeper and more mysterious. My son has been my son for eight years now. I'm somewhat ashamed to have to admit that I spent the first six of those years trying very hard to force my loud, exuberant, competitive, goofy boy into becoming a quiet, neurotic Jewish kid like I'd been. I did it with the best of motives. I wanted him to be gentle. I wanted him to do well in school. I wanted all sorts of perfectly reasonable things, but in the end, what I wanted him to be was more like me.

And this is where I get to the happy ending. This is where I say that I've come to love my son for exactly who he is. This is where I say that I've stopped looking for the volume switch to quiet Nati down, that I've come to appreciate the great multicultural mix that is my family. And there are days, more and more of them, where that's exactly true. There are days when I want nothing more than to enjoy all the laughter that Nati brings to our family. There are days when we are perfect just as we are. But it's also true that eating chicken soup with *berbere* takes a lifetime of practice. My family is as big as the globe, Ethiopian and American both, and I will, I suspect, spend the rest of my life coming to terms with what all that means.

Nati learned English very quickly. He was fluent before he'd been here a year. But then, it's easy for a father and son to speak the same words. It's learning to hear and understand them all that really takes practice.

VII.

Reflections: Children Tell Their Own Adoption Stories

I should edit a book that is completely written by children who were adopted, but I didn't realize that until I was many months into this book. The idea of children contributing to the book organically evolved as I reached out to the parents in my practice; I received news about their children, who were in some cases young adults, and I asked a few parents to invite their children to write. Here are just a few stories that are "icing on the cake" for this tender book.

Cloe was a toddler when she first arrived, and I had bonded with her parents, Diane and John Southard, while they waited to travel to China. John helped me build my first website while he was waiting to become a father. I had an early website that was hosted by AOL. It was mostly educational and became a way to grow my practice of adoption medicine in its infancy in the early

1990s. The Southards were very gracious and allowed me into their home for a TV piece about international adoption after they brought Cloe home. They were very eager to tell her story to help other parents adopting from China. I was so happy that Cloe wanted to contribute to the book. She also recently donated money she raised for Worldwide Orphans Foundation.

Huong Sutliff came to see me for the first time at Winthrop-University Hospital when she was about eight years of age. Her parents, Cindy and Cal, were my friends by the time they adopted Huong from Vietnam, and I helped them to prepare for their adoption and their trip. I love this family and we have shared a deep connection through the years. I have watched Huong grow up to be a very elegant and generous young woman, and it is hard for me to believe that she is the same little girl who spoke no English and had no understanding of American culture. Huong graduated from Poly Prep in Brooklyn having learned to be a fabulous ice-skater, an artist, a disciplined student, and a devoted daughter. She is currently in her last year at Bates College and is getting mostly all "A"s. Her story is like a painting and I love reading it out loud when I make presentations. I hope that you see the vivid scene and absorb her emotion as you read this to yourself.

Zayna Mahbub is a strikingly gorgeous Pakistani child who was adopted by Shazia and Sharyar, her devoted parents. I fell in love with her parents first during the grueling process of adoption. Since both parents are Pakistani, there was at least a reasonable process, but it was still very challenging. Once Zayna arrived in New York, I had the pleasure of being her primary-care pediatrician. She didn't like when I gave her vaccines and screamed a lot, but she forgave me finally. Her family moved to Singapore for a few years, and her parents are back in New York with a baby girl her mother gave birth to, named Anya, who you can read about in Zayna's story.

Emily Vaughan was adopted from Russia at about two years of age, and she is an artist. She loves to write and draw, and she can share her thoughts about her adoption quite articulately. Here we have a poem about her loving family (see her father, Andrew Vaughan's, story) and a fascinating interpretation of a painting. This is a small slice of her magnificent and vibrant imagination. At a very young age, Emily was able to express her feelings about her adoption.

My son Ben was born in Hanoi, Vietnam, and my son Des was born in Addis Ababa, Ethiopia. They have each visited their birth countries twice because of my work and they love their homelands. They often refer to themselves as "brothers from another mother." They wanted to be part of this book and they worked hard on their stories with no direction from me. I am proud of how they talk to each other about their past, and they are becoming more and more at ease and even humorous about their adoption stories.

CLOE SOUTHARD

Cloe Southard was born on July 25, 1995, in China, and was adopted on May 14, 1996. She lives in Long Island, New York, with her loving parents, Diane and John Southard, and is going into her junior year of high school.

May 14, 1996, is the day when everything changed. My mom flew all the way to China to get her little girl and that little girl was me. When we flew back to the United States, we landed in New York on Long Island. I got to see who my dad was when he was at the airport waiting for me. Looking back on the years, I think to myself that if I were still in China, my life would be the total opposite of what it is now.

When I was a baby on Long Island, I wasn't as healthy as I should have been. My parents took me to see Dr. Jane Aronson at Winthrop hospital. I had all kinds of tests and medication, and soon enough I was healthy. Through the years, I went to school, had playdates with my friends, and had birthday parties. My parents were very open about my adoption and my birth parents. As I was growing up, I would talk to my mom and ask her, "Do you think that my birth mom and dad ever think of me?" She always said, "I bet they never stop thinking about you. They probably think of you every day and hope that you are alive and that you have a family that loves you." And I do have a family that loves me.

On July 25, 2011, I turned sixteen and I was thinking about my birth parents more often than ever. I really don't know why, but I think that if they saw me now, I hope that they would be proud of what I've become and who I am. I've been thinking a lot about orphans as well, especially in China, where I was born. I find myself looking at pictures of children in orphanages and those wonderful people who help them. I admire those people who dedicate their lives to helping others, and I long to do that when I grow up. For now, I help in any way I can.

I have many interests, one of which is photography. I enjoy photographing people and nature and I make artistic statements. I love to do dance. It's one of my passions. For about ten years, I've been doing Chinese traditional dancing with a dance troupe at the Chinese Center on Long Island. We have danced all over the island and in parts of New York City performing ribbon, fan, and sword dances. I also dance at my school on the varsity dance team. We dance hip-hop and jazz at halftime at basketball games and other events at school. Even though I love to dance, I don't want to do it as a life career. After high school, I want to go to college and

Cloe Southard with her parents,
Diane and John Southard

major in special education, because one of my other passions is helping children with special needs. I hope to become a special education teacher some day.

When I am an adult, I want to travel around the world. I would love to go to China. I will always have a place in my heart for the country where I was born. In the meantime, I am happy and healthy, living my life with wonderful parents whom I love so much!

HUONG SUTLIFF

Huong Sutliff is a senior at Bates College studying art criticism, English, and anthropology.

MEMORIES OF A PAST AND HOPES OF A FUTURE

It was late afternoon in Hoa Binh, Vietnam, and the lush rambutan branches spilling onto the road made it hard for our driver to keep on a straight path as we approached closer to the orphanage. A flock of chickens rested near the road, pecking at the discarded remains of a star apple. Children sped by on their battered bikes. I smelled dead banana leaves soaking in a small puddle by the roadside.

The orphanage that I lived in many years ago looked abandoned. It seemed that the landscape had changed. The children were all at school; the only people there were the elderly women who had no homes and orphaned infants being nursed by young volunteers. The infants stretched their palms into the air hoping to find a tender touch. As my adoptive parents explored the various rooms, I stood in the middle of the courtyard and experienced an overwhelming feeling of melancholy. I remembered partial details of my time in Vietnam and the precise moment that my birth mother left me at the orphanage.

I was six and the day was warm. My mother had chosen to wear her most beautiful white shirt embroidered with lace detailing at the collar. I was clad in black pants, my favorite pair of turquoise sandals, and a red shirt. At the time, I didn't fully understand the extent to which her decision would impact me. I was saddened at her lack of reasoning as to why she was giving me up to the orphanage. Mostly I was frightened at the thought of losing my mother and being disconnected from my family. As I was released from her embrace, all that stood between us was the metal gate of the orphanage. She walked away and I succumbed to tears. In that moment, I hoped that she would visit me. She never did.

Visiting the orphanage where I was adopted was an emotionally difficult and complicated experience, filled with memories of disappointment but also memories that I have been able to internalize in a constructive way. Prior to my visit to Vietnam, I had no intention of returning to my orphanage in Hoa Binh for various reasons. My adoptive parents encouraged me and they accompanied me every step of the way. I found comfort in their being there. Their love and support was all that I needed to revisit my past and more important to move forward with the experiences and possibilities of the future.

ZAYNA MAHBUB

Zayna Mahbub was born on July 15, 2003, and adopted on October 17, 2003. Her baby sister is Anya.

I was adopted. At first I thought being adopted was pretty scary. It was scary because I did not know who my biological mother was. But then after having a baby sister who is not adopted, I thought about it for a long time and realized that being adopted was not so bad after all. It doesn't really matter whose tummy I came from. What matters is that I have a mother and father who adore me. When my baby sister was born, I would not stop thinking about her because I have been dying for a little sister since I was two and finally I got one!!! I love her but sometimes she can be annoying, and not just annoying, but as in rip-your-hair-out annoying!!! My sister is lucky to have me because I am her only sister in the whole wide world!

EMILY VAUGHAN

This is a painting that Emily's father bought many years ago directly from the artist. The artist was a foster father in Hempstead, New York. It was in the attic collecting dust so he offered it to Emily and hung it in her room. He asked her what she thought of it and she told him, "The mother with the green hair is dreaming about where her baby is."

By: Emily Vaughan   6/4/11

Family

Family must be importent
to you because they are always
in you heat and confert you
when you are Sad.

Family is importent to
Some peaple because they Love
you and you love them.

Family can confert you
when you are feeling down and
being Sad or lonly.

When you come off the
bus, you might see your family
waiting for you when they see
you in the window on the
bus.

THE BOY FROM HANOI

by Ben Aronson, thirteen years old

Hello, my name is Ben, and when I think about my adoption from Vietnam, I feel many feelings. I feel sad, happy, and sometimes grateful. I think about myself in the orphanage and wonder what was going on in my head.

When I am sad, I envision that I was placed on bed number 27 in the hospital in Hanoi and my mom said good-bye to me. Then she left me alone in the care of the hospital. I sometimes feel very happy about adoption because I now live in my home in Maplewood, New Jersey, with my two moms, my brother, Des, and my pet cockatiel, Rico.

I used to think that having a brother was terrible because I had to share my toys. Every night after Des went to sleep I would say to my mom, "Mama, Des stinks!" But now I feel grateful that Des came to be my big brother because he always helps and he is also very nice and loving.

These are my feelings about adoption and I hope that I have helped other adopted kids who feel the same way that I do.

LOST IN A HOTEL

by Des Aronson, fourteen years old

I was adopted from Ethiopia in May 2004 by my family from Maplewood, New Jersey. My mother, Jane Aronson, came with her foundation volunteer, Meade Barlow, who had been in Addis and visited me on many occasions. This story is about how I got lost in the Hilton Hotel in Addis Ababa, Ethiopia, in May 2004. The story was told to me by my mom and Meade and also is from my memory.

"Let's go down to breakfast," said my new mom Jane and Meade. I didn't understand a word they said until our translator, Baby, translated it for me in Amharic over the cell phone. Amharic is one of the languages spoken in Ethiopia. I was really excited about breakfast because it was going to be the first healthy and full meal I ever had. I guess that's what happens when you have a family who died of AIDS and were left to fend for yourself.

"Come on, let's go!" I yelled in Amharic. I ran ahead of them to the elevator that was around the corner from the hallway of our rooms and pressed the "down" button. I waited patiently for a little while until I heard a *ding!* I hadn't realized that Meade and my mom were so far behind, so I stepped into the elevator. I waited and waited until I saw them approaching the corner. That's when the door started to close. I stood frozen and terrified while I saw my mom and Meade try to race to the elevator door, but the door shut completely. I had no idea what to do, so I pressed all the buttons to try and open that door. The Addis Hilton is a big hotel so there were a lot of buttons.

While I stood there frozen in terror, my mom started to freak out. "How could we be so careless?" my mom said to Meade. "I just adopted him and now I lost him."

"We should've watched him more carefully," Meade replied. "But standing here talking about it won't help get him back."

"Yes, I know, but he could be on any floor by now," my Mom explained. "And to make matters worse, there are twelve floors!"

"How about I'll check floors six and down and you check floors seven and up," suggested Meade.

"Great idea, and if you find him call me and if I find him I'll call you," replied my mom.

Ding! rang the elevator door. I felt so sad and scared because once again I had lost my family. That's when I broke out into tears. *Ding!* rang the elevator door. Now I was on the seventh floor going down. When the elevator started to go down, my stomach started having butterflies and felt like it was being tossed around.

Ding! Now on the sixth floor, I decided to get off. I just stood at the front of the elevator door hoping that my mom or Meade would come through that door, but for five minutes I stood there and no one came except an elderly man murmuring words to himself.

At the same time, my mom was on the twelfth floor and began to go back down. She started to panic and called Meade to see where he was and if he had found me yet.

Ring . . . ring . . . ring! rang the phone. "Hello, Meade?" said my mom.

"Yeah, did you find Des?" answered Meade.

"No, I was hoping you had," replied my mom.

"Well . . . what floor are you on?" asked Meade.

"I am going down to the eleventh floor again," said my mom.

"Well, I am just arriving on the sixth floor . . . oh my God, I found him!" shouted Meade. "He is with me."

"Oh my God, thank you, Meade! I'll be down in a second," said my mom.

"Okay, bye," Meade replied. "Des, we have been looking everywhere for you."

I had no idea what they were saying, but I think they were relieved to see me as I was to see them. Meade gave me a big hug. That's when my mom came out of the elevator and also joined the hug. We were all united once again.

Dr. Jane and her sons dressed up as her for Halloween 2010

VIII.

The Children Left Behind

Once the adoption process has come to an end and a new family has settled, the question inevitably creeps into the minds of the parents whose lives have been blessed with a child through adoption: What about the children who were left behind?

Conditions for orphans around the world are often dire. Even in the most well-run institution with some measure of resources, nothing can replace the benefits of a permanent, nurturing home. Still, the families that have adopted children from poor countries with little resources can and do keep those children that are left behind in their hearts. Moved to see what they can do to help enrich the lives of the millions of children around the world who are still waiting in limbo or perhaps will never find stable, permanent homes, many of these adoptive families go back to their children's birth countries to lend a hand or even found their own organizations to promote the welfare of orphans around the world. In the following pages, you will hear directly from some of these parents about their dedication to the children left behind—true labors of love inspired by the adopted children who have changed their lives forever.

DEBORRA-LEE FURNESS

Deborra-lee is an actress, founder of National Adoption
Awareness Week in Australia, and board member for Worldwide
Orphans Foundation Australia. She lives with her husband, Hugh
Jackman, and children, Oscar and Ava, in New York City.

It has been several years since I began my education about the complexities of adoption. I am the extremely proud mother of two adorable, talented, gifted, mischievous (pick an adjective from the good, the bad, and the ugly), cheeky children who among many things were adopted at birth.

I have become a member of a community that is passionate about speaking out about the many children in the world who are without a family through disease, war, poverty, or extenuating circumstances. The reason I am passionate about wanting to seek an answer to solving the orphan crisis in the world is not because I have two adopted children but because I have witnessed what life is like for these kids who have nothing and no one to protect, care for, and nurture them. Adoption is one way that these kids can find a loving family and fulfill their birthright of being loved, nurtured, educated, and happy.

My journey started when my five-year-old son, Oscar, was watching TV one Saturday morning. We were flicking through the channels looking for a good cartoon and he made me stop at a World Vision advertisement that talked about how the children who lived in parts of Africa had dirty drinking water and sometimes had no mum or dad to look after them. Oscar decided he wanted to build a well for them and plant some trees so they could have fresh fruit, in particular, a lychee tree, his favorite fruit at the time.

I thought if my five-year-old son is aware enough and has the passion to want to do something, then I should step up. Through Oscar's school at the time, we ended up building a well for a small community in Kenya, and then we assisted with some other wells in Ethiopia. We visited Cambodia and sat with the street kids and witnessed how challenging their lives were too. My education had begun and along the way I met a woman who became my mentor and "partner in crime." This passionate, fierce woman with a big vision and lots of energy and the generosity of spirit to share it all is Dr. Jane Aronson.

With Dr. Jane always there in a supportive way, we have managed to bring about greater awareness for many kids in need of families. Along with some equally passionate Aussies, we created National Adoption Awareness Week (NAAW) in Australia, which has as its mission to advocate, educate, and communicate on all aspects of the adoption journey.

With this sort of awareness we can assist in getting rid of the old-fashioned stigma that surrounds adoption. We can support adoptees to navigate the subtleties of their journey and also support adoptive parents on how best to nurture their children who in many cases have come from other countries and cultures.

We continue to question our politicians on their policies so that they can continue to learn and adapt their methodologies to ensure the best practices and maintain the greatest integrity when adoption is an option. *Every child deserves a family!* My kids have taught me more than I could ever have managed on my own; they are a gift to the world.

DIANE B. KUNZ, J.D., PH.D.

Diane Kunz is executive director of the Center for Adoption Policy. A lawyer and honorary fellow of the American Academy of Adoption Attorneys and the American Academy of Assisted Reproductive Technology Attorneys, Dr. Kunz is also a historian who taught for many years at Yale and Columbia universities. She and her husband, Tom, are the parents of eight children, four of whom were born in and adopted from China.

Almost sixteen years ago, my husband, Tom, and I were in a hotel room in Wuhan, China, talking to Jane Aronson (who was a guardian angel on that trip) about our new daughter, Eleanor. The two-week adoption trip in 1996 changed our lives, Eleanor's life, and the lives of many other people.

In 1996 we were a family of six with Mom, Dad, and four biological sons, Charles, James, William, and Edward. We are now a family of eleven: same mom and dad, four biological boys, four girls (Eleanor, sixteen, Sarah, eleven, Catherine, nine, and Elizabeth, seven) adopted from China, and Inna, our daughter-in-law. Obviously our family is at the center of our adoption story, but it is not just about them.

Adoption was a means of creating our family, but it has also become a passion that has changed my professional life just as it has changed the lives of so many adoptive parents. At the time we adopted Eleanor, I was teaching diplomatic history at Yale. Since then, I have cofounded a not-for-profit, Center for Adoption Policy (CAP), the aim of which is to remove barriers to international and domestic adoption. We know that not every orphan or vulnerable child will have a family, but we believe that ethical and transparent adoption practices can and must remain a viable method for family creation. Simultaneously, I returned to the practice of law (my first career) with a specialty in adoption law.

Ann Reese, whose children were also patients of Dr. Jane Aronson, is the co–executive director of CAP. We have worked on legislation and research and have annually hosted the Adoption Law and Policy Conference at New York Law School. We bring diplomats and experts together from all over the world, as well as birth parents, adoptive parents, and adoptees, to discuss issues relating to international and domestic adoption.

We have educated government agencies about specific adoption advocacy/legal issues and participated in the dramatic Special Humanitarian Parole Program for Haitian Orphans which paroled 1,100 children who were previously in the process of being adopted by U.S. families to the United States in an expedited manner.

We chaired meetings that drafted the documents allowing Haitian adoptees to receive finalized adoption decrees in U.S. courts; we made the rounds to congressional offices to explain why they should support the Help HAITI Act of 2010, which granted these children green cards and a desperately needed pathway to citizenship. The day President Obama signed Help HAITI into law was the greatest day for the Haitian children who were adopted by their families and for those who spent months working toward this goal.

Millions of orphans need families and we cannot ignore their perilous position. Worldwide Orphans Foundation, Half the Sky, Love Without Boundaries, and many other orphan support organizations are doing great work enriching the lives of children living without families in their communities around the world. CAP advocates for orphans in another direction; we work with the U.S. Department of State, USCIS (U.S. Citizens and Immigration Services), USAID (U.S. Agency for International Development), and diplomats in countries abroad to maintain and improve international adoption programs. The answer to bad practices in international adoption is not to shut down country programs but to punish the perpetrators. If adoption practices are not perfect, then we should fix them instead of ending adoption opportunities for innocent children.

I have also been a source of education and support to families seeking to adopt and to those families who, for various reasons, have been unable to obtain the necessary visa to bring their child to the United States. Politics and foreign affairs can disrupt a multilateral quest to be parents. My family and I lived through a U.S. government shutdown, Taiwan testing missiles, 9/11, SARS, and swine flu, to name a few. There still remain viable international adoption programs that can be found on some websites, such as the Joint Council on International Children's Services at www .jointcouncil.org.

My family has hosted two Chinese graduate students at Duke University. We met Hui and his wife, Wei, almost seven years ago when we first moved to Durham, North Carolina. We were in a similar position as mothers-to-be. Wei was pregnant with her daughter Lin, and Tom and I were waiting for travel approval so we could bring our daughter Elizabeth home from China. We have all become very close. Last night I was honored to participate as an honorary parent in Hui's very moving Ph.D. hooding ceremony.

Since they are only moving to Columbus, Ohio, we feel sure that we will keep in touch. We would never have had this meaningful relationship had we not adopted Eleanor.

As we were driving away from the Duke auditorium after the graduation, Wei reminded me that her mother, who since has passed away, had come from China and visited our home and met my daughters. Wei said, "My mother believes that Chinese people have previous lives. She said that your girls must have been very good in their previous lives because that is why they ended up adopted by you." We feel that prior good in past lives is a very fine way of describing the incomparable blessings we have had since that October day in Wuhan so many years ago.

ELLORA DECARLO COOPER

Ellora DeCarlo Cooper resides in New York City with her husband, Gary, and three children, Julia, Leo, and Lorenzo. She is the president and cofounder of Futuro de los Niños and one of the founding members of the Guatemala 900.

I wanted to adopt a child internationally for as long as I could remember. There was just something in my heart that told me this was my future path. I had no idea how to begin this adventure or what lay in store for me, my husband, and the children who have become the heart of our home, Julia, Leo, and Lorenzo.

After two years of completing, renewing, and re-renewing our home study, my husband, Gary, and I finally stopped dragging our feet and took a trip to Guatemala. We wanted to get a feel for the country, the culture, and the children who needed a family. Once again, we had no idea of the life-altering journey that lay before us.

While in Guatemala we volunteered with Habitat for Humanity and had the opportunity to see much of the country and visit a few children's homes. The beauty and warmth of the people juxtaposed against extreme poverty and heartbreaking conditions opened our eyes to a world outside our own. We were hooked! We left Guatemala with referrals for two beautiful children, both six weeks old at the time, and our hearts were heavy knowing the dreaded waiting period was about to begin. I was never even sure I had that "mothering" instinct that everyone talked about, but it bit me in the butt like I couldn't believe, and I was instantly ready to start some serious *mothering*!

When we first arrived home after our visit, we immersed ourselves in the necessary paperwork and preparations, but I couldn't move forward as I felt I should because something kept me awake at night crying and feeling totally incomplete. With the threat of the closing of all adoptions in Guatemala on the horizon, we knew that many of the children we met on our trip would not have a family of their own. Three weeks later, we flew back to Guatemala and accepted a referral for a third child. And so it began.

People always ask me, "Did you intend to adopt three children at the same time? How did it happen?" I wish I had the answer! Gary and I knew we couldn't stop, and we figured we would just go for it and work it out later; we are still operating by this creed today. Our life is as full, chaotic, joyous, tumultuous, exhausting, and lovely as you might expect!

We visited the children once a month, as did many of our friends and family. We were able to take them to our hotel, and after four nights (six to seven wake-ups per night), hundreds of "poopie" diapers, and dozens of bottles, we would fly home exhausted and heartbroken after returning them to their orphanage until the next visit. After seven months of this routine, with no end in sight, Gary and I decided to move to Guatemala to foster the children and finish out their adoptions. Days before our move, the orphanage was raided by the government and they tried to remove all fifty-one children from the only home they had ever known, where they were safe and loved. A Guatemalan court order required that they remain in the home, and we were never able to take them out again until they came home almost a year later.

After five of my darkest months visiting the children daily, Gary and I moved into the orphanage to live as a family among the forty-eight other orphaned and abandoned children of Semillas de

Amor. We were accepted and embraced by our tiny neighbors and indoctrinated about orphan culture. Most of what I live by today comes from the lessons learned while living with these small wise souls. Sleeping on the floor with no running water or electricity proved easier than this spoiled New Yorker could have ever imagined. I was a mother and protector to my small vulnerable brood.

The children's home was unjustly harassed and adoptions were stalled; we needed emergency funding to support the fifty-one children who remained. There wasn't enough money to pay the caregivers and many days not enough food to feed the kids. Gary and I partnered with the orphanage director, Nancy Bailey, to keep the home intact and the children safe. This was the beginning of our foundation, Futuro de los Niños, which continues to help support Semillas de Amor Children's Village today.

In the spring of 2009, after eighteen months of waiting to be a family, all of our children's adoptions were finalized and they were able to come home. We were lucky. Within months of returning home, we began to mobilize many of the families whose children were still trapped in Guatemala in what had become a bureaucratic nightmare. This was the inception of the Guatemala 900, a grass-roots campaign advocating for the children and families caught between the old and new law and a fierce political agenda.

Today we estimate over four hundred children whose adoptions still languish remain in Guatemala. Thirty children remain at Semillas de Amor, and fifteen of them have waiting families. Some days I watch my children laugh, play, learn, and thrive and my heart is full of happiness knowing they are safe and free. On many days, I look at their sweet faces and wonder why so many parents and children are still suffering, living thousands of miles apart, their future as a family still uncertain.

Futuro de los Niños foundation and Guatemala 900 are a legacy of our family's journey and the gifts we have received from the children of Guatemala. We made a promise to the orphans who have touched our hearts that we will never forget them or stop fighting for them to have the bright future they deserve!

Lorenzo, Julia, and Leo DeCarlo Cooper

TERRY BAUGH

Terry Baugh is president and cofounder of Kidsave International, working to give one million orphans and kids in foster care adoptive families and lifelong connections with adults by 2020. Terry is the parent of three children adopted from Russia and lives and works in Washington, D.C.

I didn't plan it, but somewhere along the way, adoption became my passion and my life. It is the kids who fuel my passion. In the dead center of every adoption is a child whose life took a terrible turn for the worse when they lost their parents. The children have no control over adult circumstances, and if the child ends up in an orphanage, this fuels long-term neglect. It is not possible for a child to really thrive without a parent.

I had traveled to some of the world's poorest countries before setting out on my own Russian adoption trip. I saw street children in Egypt, India, Morocco, Algeria, and the Philippines. They were cute ragamuffins living in extreme poverty, begging for money and carousing in packs. This didn't prepare me for what I saw in a Russian orphanage. There were rows of beds, children eating in groups, and toddlers with shaved heads sitting (not toddling) in a playpen with no toys and no stimulation. Children appeared comatose, robot-like, pale, and listless.

My identified child, Dasha, was adorable in her photo, and by twelve months of age, she had lived in a hospital, then an orphanage, and then was transferred to another orphanage because the first one didn't believe in international adoption. The orphanage I toured was a big, cold building with about fifty-five other children and too few caretakers. While I was there, we had grave concerns that Dasha might be mentally retarded because her medical abstract stated that she suffered from hypothyroidism and a scary Russian diagnosis called "perinatal encephalopathy." In spite of warnings from the U.S. pediatrician, I was incapable of walking away. The orphanage had drugged her with phenobarbital to force her to stop crying; no wonder she seemed mentally retarded. It was a crapshoot whether this little girl would be okay, but I realized that I would rather parent a severely mentally retarded child than abandon her. I could not walk away and I took her home.

I met my second daughter, Luda, three years later when she was just two years old. She had been abandoned because of a birth defect that was "a gaping hole" in her lip and palate. Her nose and teeth were deformed, and she was officially diagnosed with bilateral cleft lip and palate that was unrepaired and covered with a bandage. I guess the deformity scared her birth mother into leaving her in the hospital. In 1993, children with clefts were considered mentally incompetent, and the money to fix such a physical problem was impossible for a Russian family. So little Luda was left alone in a maternity hospital to fend for herself. When I met her, she had been so neglected she didn't know how to be held. She arched her back when I picked her up rather than drawing her body to mine as any other child would do instinctively. She haunted me until I adopted her. It took a year and a half to make it all happen.

Kost, my third child, was healthy as a little horse. He spent seven years in a Russian orphanage because his alcoholic parents had lost their rights to parent their eleven children. I met Kost on a KidSave Summer Miracles trip that gives groups of orphans the opportunity to spend time in a family setting and meet families interested in adoption. He stayed at our house and demonstrated what modest neglect looked like in a ten-and-a-half-year-old. He could read and write, but his back was full of knots from years of lack of touch and never enough hugs. His main words were "Watch me, watch me." He delighted in having someone pay attention. While he had two loving sisters in the orphanage with him who did their best to watch out for him, he lacked the nurturing that a parent provides. Orphanage caregivers aren't monsters, but they are usually overworked women with too many mouths to feed, too many kids to manage, and no training.

Erika was a little girl I thought I could protect in my home, but some abuse is too tough for love and patience to overcome. Erika's abuse was at the hands of her birth mother, her grandmother, and a foster parent. She didn't make it in her first adoptive home and she didn't make it in mine either. While she was removed from her culture for adoption, I remedied that error, returning her to a place where she could feel safe. While I am not able to parent her, she is now stable in a loving home environment with a caring mother who is focused on her success.

What children need are caring adults in their lives who focus only on them. Staff in a fity-five-person orphanage, a twenty-person orphanage, and even an eight-person group home have a hard time doing this. This is not their commitment. The need for a caring adult in a child's life is such a no-brainer, but most people don't think about orphans. Together Dasha, Luda, Kost, and I make up a family. They are all smart, productive young adults now. There was lots of therapy and arguments and movies and family engagement along the way. Their time with me has flown. Dasha is clearly not mentally retarded. She attends an honors college. Luda is facing her last reconstructive surgery to realign her jaw; she has had fifteen years of treatment and she is almost done. She's a popular, athletic teen preparing for college admissions. Kost is in college studying computer security and working, sometimes two jobs. His biological sisters were able to leave the orphanage too, so pieces of his birth family remain intact and connected to ours.

My adoption experiences led me to start KidSave, a nonprofit organization that helps older children find adoptive parents and lasting connections. We also advocate for and support governments to create change for at-risk kids who need families. Just last week I heard stories of three children who have had miraculous opportunities because an adult stepped up to help. A boy in U.S. foster care who thought he would grow up to be a gangbanger now has a caring family and wants to attend medical school. A Colombian boy whose parents sold him into slavery ran away when he had the chance and ended up with a single dad in Los Angeles. A Kazakh teen saw her grandfather brutally murdered when she was three years of age. She was adopted, and after years of guilt for loving her adoptive mom and not saving her biological family, she realized there was a divine hand in her life because she ended up with a good family in Los Angeles.

Adoption takes complex, tragic, and ugly social situations where kids are victims and creates loving families. Nothing could be more of a miracle.

DIANE HARAPIN

*Diane Harapin is an educator and has been working with
National Adoption Awareness Week (NAAW) in Australia for
five years. She lives in Sydney with her husband, Paul, and their
four young children, one of whom is Nathan (Sathia), who was
adopted from Cambodia.*

This special journey began when my husband, Paul, and I moved
to Singapore for work in 1998. While in Singapore, we traveled
throughout Asia enjoying the cultures of Malaysia, China, Indone-
sia, and Thailand. It was an exciting and adventurous period of our
lives and led us to the extraordinary experience of adopting our
son, Sathia.

After working full-time and studying for my second master's
degree part-time, I enjoyed being part of an expatriate community.
I was working in the information technology industry and became
involved with a group who held fund-raisers for Cambodian orphanages and donated vital items such as first-aid supplies and
toys for the kids. I also had friends at the Australian school in
Singapore who were going to Cambodia to build houses, teach
English, and work in orphanages. These projects are now known
as service holidays and are becoming more popular; back then it
was a unique way to spend vacation time.

After suffering a miscarriage and trying to conceive for two
years, we decided to join our friends on their Cambodia trip. I
could teach English and we could investigate adoption. What
started as a four-day trip turned into a lifelong relationship with

our gorgeous son, Sathia. Our interest in adoption had a long history, and we dreamed about it when we were in our early twenties, backpacking through India and staying next to an orphanage. We loved the kids at the orphanage, and at the ripe old age of twenty, we talked about our strong desire to become a family through adoption.

Eight hours after we arrived in Phnom Penh, we went to visit Sathia because he was supposed to have been adopted by a woman I knew and the adoption was unsuccessful. We really wanted to meet him, and once we met him we fell in love. He was the happiest and most beautiful baby I had ever seen. He had a terrible facial skin infection, his skull was dented at the back, and he had a severely turned eye. We thought he was the most gorgeous person we had ever laid eyes on. He was only eight weeks old and very chubby, much chubbier than the kids we saw in the orphanages, and well looked after by a nurse and her sister. When I held him I thought, this is my son! It is hard to explain and certainly not something I could have envisioned, but there he was, my boy, in a hammock, in an old apartment building with no lights, in Cambodia. I had only been in Cambodia for eight hours and I had decided to do everything I could to be the mother of little Sathia.

Throughout the days one of us would volunteer at the main orphanage in Phnom Penh, supposedly one of the cleaner and well-staffed orphanages, and one of us would visit Sathia and take him for short walks while navigating the world of intercountry adoption and its paperwork.

As a young woman, I had no concept of orphanages; the closest I had come to orphaned children was watching UNICEF and World Vision ads out of the corner of my eye and trying not to be too affected or feel too sorry for them. Having been a teacher, I loved the idea of working with kids in care, but being there was the most life-changing and personally inspiring opportunity.

The conditions in the orphanage were very poor, and the over-crowding and myriad health issues still make me cry when I think of them some twelve years later. Most of the babies were just lying on the floor; some were profoundly disabled, some seemed so sad, and some smelled from being soiled for so long. It seemed everyone had lice and skin sores, and some even had open wounds with para-sites inside the wounds. They needed so many more "nannies," but there was no money to employ them.

The nannies were trying hard to attend to everyone, but it was so hot, humid, and overcrowded that it was impossible. The nap-pies were cheap pieces of old cloth, and most of the soiled ones were just heaped in a corner covered in flies and waiting to be cleaned. There were very few toys. Our donated toys seemed to have been taken from the children, and we were told to open the tins of formula to be sure they would be given to the babies and not sold on the black market. The rules of the West do not apply here, and being extremely poor leads to desperate acts. Every day a few babies came in and ended up being adopted by European and American couples and some single parents.

I was told the older children in the orphanage very seldom get adopted and are labeled "unadoptable"; they stay until they are about twelve years of age and have to earn their own living. The streets were full of very young children, some as young as three years old, selling things to tourists and, of course, many child beg-gars. The amount of children in prostitution is apparently stagger-ing, as is the amount of child slaves. It is a very tough place to be born. The street children were adorable, but in order to survive they had to be very cunning, and they all had a deep sadness in their eyes.

Once you enter the orphanage the older kids come up to you and start smiling. Some ask for you to adopt them and say in perfect English, "I love you, can I be your son?" It is heart-wrenching and something that haunts me today. Philosophically, I recognized that they just needed a family and deserved a family.

We then proceeded to adopt Sathia under the laws of Cambodia and Singapore. We employed lawyers in both countries and translators to translate all documents into Khmer, Mandarin, and English. The process involved a lot of paperwork, including an Interpol clearance, a psychological assessment, personal financial records, pay slips, copies of our degrees, and personal and professional references. We had to provide photos of us, our home, and our extended family and have them all notarized by a lawyer. Sathia's Australian citizenship required months of waiting, and while we waited, we had to remain in Singapore. We came home to Australia once and had to leave before his visa expired in case he "overstayed" his visa and became an illegal immigrant, even though we were Australians and he was legally our son!

Our son is now twelve years old and a fantastic person; he is social, smart, athletic, and very funny. He says he is both Australian and a Cambodian Khmer. He plays Australian rules football, a strange game unfamiliar to most of the world, with much talent and moves between the cultures of his birth and his new country. He is learning Khmer and loves going to the Buddhist temple. Recently, he visited his homeland and loved being "just like everybody else." He felt powerful when Cambodian strangers spoke to him in Khmer. We recognize that being in a transracial family has its complexities, and so we will continue to support Sathia's visits to his birth country and answer all his questions as best we can; we will ask for support from adult adoptees, adoptive families, and specialists in this area. We are blessed we found our son in Cambodia and would love if more people could adopt Cambodian children. In fact, we wish all orphans from anywhere in the world would be adopted, because they need a family.

Now we sit on several boards working with children's advocacy and adoption. Our journey has led us to support the work of our patron at National Adoption Awareness Week, Deborra-lee Jackman, an adoptive mum and child advocate. She is an inspiration to us all as she fights for the rights of children and reminds us that "every child deserves a family" and we are all valuable.

I have also formed a special friendship with a lovely, articulate, and passionate pediatrician and supporter of the lonely and lost children of the world, Dr. Jane Aronson. We are kindred spirits, and from across the world, I read her words and feel her passion as she reminds us that we have so much great work to do together to help children at risk.

My volunteer work for Australia's National Adoption Awareness Week supports children around the world who need a family, and adoptees and their families. I fight for those we left behind all those years ago in Cambodia; I fight for my son's right to be in a loving family and to grow up healthy and safe. I know it may not be possible for every child to have a family, but I work to support organizations that assist kids to achieve their potential and to provide best practices in adoption in Australia.

LAURA HOGE

Laura Hoge is a songwriter who lives in High Bridge, New Jersey, with her husband and daughter adopted from Rwanda.

HOPE AND THE BLUE DOORS

Almost two years into our adoption process, a friend of mine sent me a picture of the main gate at Home of Hope orphanage in Kigali, Rwanda. The doors were large, metal, and deep blue. For two years prior, I had felt completely trapped by a madness that is impossible to describe without truly experiencing it. The ebb and flow of hope and despair was unpredictable at best, and I would find myself fortified with optimism for long stretches of time, only to be doubled over in a visceral moan without warning. I did not know how much more I would be able to survive.

While it was difficult for me to imagine my child behind this gated entrance, largely because of the fear of setting myself up for the pain of an adoption failure, I began to visualize a small bird flying freely back and forth over a royal blue gate. I pictured my little friend chirping lullabies to the children when they arrived, carefully helping to tuck them in at night with its small beak, and singing psalms along with the Sisters of Charity during their morning prayers. I read Emily Dickinson's poem "Hope"—"Hope is the thing with feathers"—until my anthology was weather worn, and I found solace in knowing that this little bird would never leave me and would never leave my child, in spite of the many circumstances that remained out of our control.

In my darkest hours, I would take this visualization even further and write songs of my own, then in my mind's eye watch my bird carry them across the sea and up over the big blue doors to where the children were sleeping. "There's a light, and it shines across the water," I would sing. "There's a light, and it carries me where you are. Let it shine across the water to your heart." Sometimes I would fingerpick on my guitar, crooning softly in the middle of the night, and sometimes I would strum loudly, whistling happily between the chorus and the melody. Oftentimes I would sing by the window, where my husband hung a bird feeder for me on a day when my sadness seemed interminable. I would imagine the grosbeaks and the chickadees dancing along to the melody before collecting sunflower seeds and flying off into the vast horizon.

The journey to find our daughter came to a magical end on May 2, 2011. It was that day that my husband and I first caught a glimpse of the large blue doors of Home of Hope orphanage in Kigali. As they began to open, I could feel myself letting go of the longing and pain of the prior two and a half years. In its place I welcomed optimism and possibility, happiness and future, and a fierce commitment to the resilient and patient soul who had already become the best part of me.

While I do not often revisit the agony I felt during those years of waiting, I am often reminded of the hope that sustained me through it all. I felt it the very moment they put her in my arms. I saw it in her eyes when she took her first steps. I continue to watch it cast a glow across her face every time she sees a bird on the feeder, which now hangs outside her bedroom window. *"Tweet!*

Tweet!" she says, and I think it's the most beautiful sound in the world.

I imagine it collecting on the wind and carrying across the sea, up over the big blue doors of the orphanage, bringing comfort and hope to the children who are still waiting.

Hoge family

MARY BACON

Mary is an actress, and her husband, Andrew Leynse, is the
artistic director of Primary Stages theater. They live with their
terrific son in New York City.

Our story began at a restaurant in Brooklyn in October 2009. We
were talking with friends who, with the help of an adoption agency,
had just entered Ethiopia's adoption program. I had recently heard
stories about Ethiopia from my dear friend Lisa, who had spent
the previous summer working in Addis Ababa, Ethiopia, with Dr.
Jane Aronson, founder and CEO of Worldwide Orphans Foundation. Lisa was assisting her to create a summer arts camp program
that Jane wanted to provide for students at the new WWO Academy that would serve many orphanages in Addis Ababa. Lisa had
a simply marvelous time, and she fell in love with the kids, the
wondrous country, and the spirit and beauty of the Ethiopians she
came to know.

Jump to us that October night. As we talked to our friends
Jenn and Steve, we found ourselves drawn to Ethiopian adoption in a way that adopting domestically or from China had not.
I have no idea why, but we just felt pulled. I think we made our
first phone call to the agency our friends were using within the
week.

That spring, we compiled our dossier for U.S. approval. And
then in June, it was off to Ethiopia to hopefully be granted the
country's approval. We were officially put on the waiting list for a

referral, and told that the average wait was seven to eight months. All of it felt pretty abstract to me, and I had a hard time believing that so much paperwork would eventually lead to a child.

Lisa called me that same June. She was going back to work at Camp Addis in July, and she thought I'd be interested. I jumped at a chance to possibly get to know Ethiopia. I asked if I could assist her or WWO in any way; basically, could I tag along? I was accepted by WWO as an extra hand for Lisa and the group of Global Arts Rangers all preparing for Camp Addis. I had never traveled farther than Europe or Mexico, and I had never been on a flight that lasted more than six hours. But still, I was going.

The experience blew my mind. Ethiopia is challenging, confusing, and amazing. Camp was held at the school. The facilities were humble, but the spirit was infectious. Necessity was the mother of invention there. I worked with six- to nine-year-old orphans. The children were affectionate, bright, and eager. We used mats in the classrooms, and we used the asphalt yard for games and soccer.

I spent wonderful, warm moments with the humble cooks and cleaners of the school in the back kitchen. Lisa brought Rit dye to make tie-dye shirts, which were completely unheard of to the cooks and cleaners. They brought their sheets from home to tie-dye too. My favorite Ethiopian meals were at the camp. The cooks used a small wood fire in the back, cutting up carrots and cabbage for the best *gomen* (chopped collard greens simmered in a mild sauce of oil, onion, and herbs) I have ever tasted. They also made *injera* (a very thin bread/pancake), fermenting it and pouring it out on large flat ovens that I've never seen anywhere else.

Camp Addis also hired adolescent orphans as counselors, kids who had grown up in Addis's orphanage system, the "organization," as my soon-to-be dear friend Abraham referred to it. They taught me much more than I could ever teach them. They were hard-working, they took nothing for granted, and their hearts were open. They were our interpreters, as well as a vital link between the young children and the faculty, and the children grew very close to their "big brothers and big sisters." I taught acting to kids who didn't know what a play was, and often found myself wondering if they needed this information as much as they needed shoes and an education. But I was met with love and appreciation for whatever I was able to do for them. My previous fears about adopting from this country disappeared. I found myself connecting with people I never would've gotten to know had I not worked for WWO. A few are my friends for life.

Dr. Sophie Mengistu, the country director for WWO in Ethiopia, oversees all of its programs, including a large family HIV/AIDS clinic as part of her tenacious fight for the care of HIV-positive orphans. She told me this when I asked her how she felt about Americans adopting kids from Ethiopia: "Mary, I have millions of orphans here. Every child deserves two loving parents. These kids, if they are adopted, will one day return to Ethiopia. That is good for our country."

I learned much I didn't know. I learned that adoption is a small fix for any country's orphan problem. WWO's purpose is to help the majority of orphans for whom adoption is not a possibility develop into proud citizens of their country. I had come to Camp Addis to get to know Ethiopia, but now I felt part of a much greater effort. I found myself grateful to be able to contribute the little I did.

My experience gave me context and insight for what our

adoption would entail. Our first referral came in January 2010 for a gorgeous little boy. On the day of the court hearing, though, the adoption fell through. The family information was inaccurate, the proper prior investigation hadn't occurred, and he was ineligible for adoption. Poverty, miscommunication, and the painful situations that make this proud country unable to care for its own children were the root causes for what went wrong in our case. Ethiopia is presently struggling to implement and ensure ethical and transparent adoptions. My experience in the country, as well as the invaluable counsel of Dr. Jane Aronson and Tom DiFilipo, the president of the Joint Council on International Children's Services (both of whom are adoptive parents themselves), helped my husband and I understand what happened and how to proceed.

Dr. Aronson said, "What happened to you is not uncommon. Hopefully it will improve for future Ethiopian adoptions. In the meantime, you got into this process to get a baby. Get another baby. And if the first little boy becomes adoptable at a later date, then you can have two." We followed her direction and asked to be matched as soon as possible with another child.

On May 15, 2010, we got our second referral. We were both home that morning; we opened our e-mail together and called our caseworker. We saw photos of a tiny, sweet, wide-eyed one-month-old boy. He was born on my mother's birthday, April 2. He was five weeks old, and he had been in our agency's care since day two.

His given name is Abadi, which means "someone who brings comfort in bad times and makes you forget your sorrow." We were struck by this, feeling bereft after losing the first child. We began to hope little Abadi might really be meant for us.

Next we hoped for a coveted court date prior to the court's summer closing, but we weren't granted one. As it happened, though, my mother became terminally ill over the summer and passed away in early August. Had we been in Ethiopia in July meeting Abadi, I wouldn't have been able to spend the last month of life with her. She saw the video of him that my former colleague from Camp Addis took on a special trip to assist the school. He made a trip to see Abadi for me, along with Abraham and Terefe, who was my unofficial driver while I was in Addis as a Global Arts Ranger.

Things seemed to be working out through cosmic logic that I can only recognize now, in hindsight. Serendipitously, we met Abadi very soon after losing my mom. We traveled to Ethiopia for our court date on October 12. Abadi had just turned six months old. During that week of court appointments and visits with Abadi, I was reunited with friends at the WWO Academy. I brought my husband, Andrew, to all the places I'd told him about, and I introduced him to the people who were so dear to me. He got to see Ethiopia through the eyes of people who worked and lived there, just as I had hoped.

Terefe picked us up at the airport and served as our driver during the court week, as well as during our second week with Abadi. He navigated us through court and visited Abadi with us daily. He served not only as our translator for all of our interactions but also as our guide to the culture and the pulse and the rhythm of the country.

When we finally met little Abadi for the first time, it was with ten or so other fellow babies who were all sunning diaperless on a large blanket in the yard of the agency's care center. Some were laid out like movie stars, and the air was filled with laughing and cooing. Abadi was nervous, sweet, and had a delicious belly laugh and dimples. He was perfectly himself. The idea that someone we knew only through photographs could make us fall in love so ferociously over a few short days filled us with wonder.

Terefe made it possible for us to spend valuable time in the nursery with Abadi, enabling us to know the women who had been caring for him every day. We hung out and chatted and laughed. We learned about Abadi but also about the caretakers in the orphanage. Our son will know that we met the people who took care of him and who imparted love, sweetness, and joy. We intend to bring Abadi to visit them on our future trips to Addis. I feel lucky that Abadi is from Ethiopia, where loving, caring, and affectionate children are at the heart of the country's culture. I will always be thankful for the love, spice, and dignity that Ethiopia has shown me.

Seven months later, we are still engrossed in the Abadi story; that strong little force is growing and laughing every day. He has become trusting and affectionate with us, and while he retains his reserve when being introduced to anything new, he also has a curiosity and a sharpness we noticed during our first visits in the nursery in Addis. He has two teeth coming in and laughs a full belly laugh every day. We are bonding and getting used to each other as a family of three.

Our Ethiopian experience that preceded bringing Abadi home has made us bigger, more aware, and more compassionate people who are determined to help if we can. Abadi has made us "part Ethiopian," and we are lucky to feel that significance. We assume over time that our commitment will deepen as we remain connected to the country. Terefe and Abraham regularly keep in touch, and I hope to bring Abadi to Camp Addis one day. I hope that my work in Ethiopia and our adoption will have helped the country in some way.

Abadi has fulfilled our dream as parents. We are the lucky ones.

More than anything, I think adoption has taught us about the vast capacity of the human heart to love all that is outside itself.

I cannot imagine how I would have learned that in any other way.

Thank you, Ethiopia. Thank you, WWO and Camp Addis.

JUSTIN D. BURTON, PH.D.

Justin Burton teaches music history in New Jersey, where he lives with his wife, Kathryn, who is a social worker. They are the proud parents of Emmett Adu, who was adopted from Ethiopia, and is now four years old, tall, happy, and very into basketball and counting.

THE PICTURE

There's a picture next to the computer monitor in my basement where I do a lot of my work when I am at home. It's the first picture I saw of my son with his eyes open.

We got an excited call one afternoon, and a picture followed. We saw a tiny, tired little guy with his eyes shut, arms and legs splayed, being held up by two anonymous hands. We loved that picture, printed it, and handed it out to everyone in the family. But we wanted more.

It would be eight weeks before we would travel. A few other groups were going before us, though, so we perused the Listservs and found other adoptive parents to request photos. Several obliged, but after a few weeks, we had only accumulated more pictures of our sleeping son.

Finally, just two weeks before we traveled, we received three pictures with the following message:

"Here are a few pics—he was ALWAYS asleep but the nanny

was so sweet that one day when I was in the courtyard and he was awake she came running out to get me to take his picture."

There were three in the set, and the third is the one that is framed next to our computer. He is wearing plaid shorts and a hoodie that reads KENNEBUNKPORT MAINE, with the aforementioned nanny cradling him. We finally saw those wonderful eyes and melted for the first of many times.

THE ANGEL

For all of our longing to see his eyes in those pictures, my focus has actually always been drawn to the nanny, Ammara, holding him in her arms. She is smiling, and she looks proud. I remember seeing that photo for the first time and suddenly feeling very safe knowing that Ammara was looking after our son.

One of the stories in the Hebrew Bible tells of Abraham during one of his more problematic moments, but it's a story that manages to end in one of the most beautiful ways I can imagine. He has hastily coupled with Sarah's handmaiden, Hagar, and Sarah becomes jealous of both Hagar and Hagar's son by Abraham, Ishmael. Abraham takes the cowardly way out and banishes Hagar and Ishmael. Hagar quickly runs out of water and fears for her son's life before she encounters an angel in the wilderness who ministers to them. Stranded far from home, unable to care for themselves, Hagar and Ishmael found comfort in the arms of a stranger.

After he was placed in the orphanage, but before he knew us, our son was in a bureaucratic wilderness. We waited for thirteen court dates to pass, for visas to be issued, for immigration papers to be approved, for two governments separated by thousands of miles and multiple language barriers to meticulously grind out the particulars of an ethical adoption. And all the while, our son was stuck in limbo without us.

But there were angels in that wilderness. There were men and women who attended to his every need and who loved him when the two families who were desperate to love him could not be with him. In the absence of any other faces, Ammara quickly came to represent everyone who was caring for our little boy. Her name, her face, and her smile comprised the embodiment of the angel in our son's wilderness.

THE UPSHOT

We eventually met Ammara and many of the other Ethiopian people who cared for our son during those crucial months when he was without both of his families. I know that she's a person, not a metaphor, and I know that she didn't work alone in keeping Adu healthy and emotionally strong. I also know the dangers of essentialisms, which reduce real people to crude caricatures.

When I look at that picture next to my computer screen, I can't help but think of Ammara as the angel, not just in my son's wilderness, but in every wilderness. She has come to symbolize everything that I trust in a world where resources are divided up so unfairly, creating no access to the most basic resources to ensure that children can stay with their birth families. In an unjust world, Ammara does exemplary work by any moral or ethical code; her caretaking of children she doesn't know provides them with an opportunity to be safe when they otherwise would have become very sad and afraid.

We'll spend a lifetime helping our son connect our family to his first family, telling him of the great trust and terrible sacrifice that his first family made on his behalf. And we'll also tell him about those few months between families when he encountered Ammara. We'll point to the picture by the computer and show him the woman who cradled him when his two families could not. She is the angel who has come to embody that which he can trust about the world around him.

Epilogue

Through all the years of international adoption, it has stalled, sputtered, and surged, and most seasoned adoption professionals have become accustomed to its fits and starts. After all, there was so much good happening. I never really imagined that I wouldn't be busy examining new babies every week in my New York office. Adoption is a deep and meaningful way to create families and provides orphans and vulnerable children with a permanent, protected, safe, and secure environment in which to recover, grow, and thrive. That is what kids deserve. And yet, the "golden age" of international adoption was nearing its end, cemented by the Hague Convention on Intercountry Adoption in 2008. As the numbers of adoptions decreased, I gradually downsized my pediatric practice. This downsizing coincided with the growth of my foundation, Worldwide Orphans Foundation. WWO serves the increasing numbers of orphans in institutions and extremely poor communities abroad, working to help them to become healthy, independent, productive members of their communities and the world.

In 2004, international adoptions to the United States peaked at 22,991, with countries like Russia, China, Guatemala, and South Korea leading the way. Unfortunately, over the last eight years, that number plummeted to 8,668 in 2012, according to the U.S. State Department's Office of Children's Affairs. These numbers represent a tragic historic moment in adoption that is marked by monumental losses for families and children.

Parents who are hoping to adopt today must struggle with extremely limited choices in terms of open countries. Meanwhile, politics make hostages of orphans in almost every sending country, and I know that, for a long time, I became adept at denying the gravity of these closures. Some countries closed their doors with drama and media coverage that made me cringe. I despised and feared adoption articles in magazines and newspapers. If the title wasn't ugly, accusatory, and misleading, the content was most definitely written with a bias that would create distrust and fear around adoption. Yet many of the stories are true—Cambodia was one country that closed with an adoption agency owner going to jail. Guatemala summarily shut down and left hundreds of families mid-process; now there are "super" orphanages in Guatemala where kids are warehoused and abused. Ethiopia recently has slowed to a crawl in the United States and has closed entirely in Australia because of accusations of trafficking. Today, the length of time it takes to complete an international adoption of a healthy baby from China to the United States can be as long as seven years. Special-needs programs have helped families fast-track adoptions in China and other countries, but it can still take years.

In 2009, when a newly adopted little boy from Russia was put on a plane to Russia alone by his adoptive mother, everyone thought that Russia would close, but advocacy prevailed and it remained open, though on the brink of closure. This was a reckless act of abandonment, and, in retrospect, was not an isolated event. There were nineteen Russian adoptees allegedly killed by their American parents during the years I was practicing adoption medicine (see the infamous Renee Polreis case in Colorado). Russian adoption was finally banned by the Russian government at the end of 2012 due to fragile Russian–American government politics. Currently, open programs include Taiwan, South Korea, Ethiopia, Congo, China, and a smattering of other countries. That said, the numbers are abysmally low and the process is long and excruciating.

Trafficking of orphans and paying off birth mothers is impossible to fathom. It is not as rampant as the media and others report, but even one child and one family affected by trafficking is unbearable to think about. Unfortunately, our fear and loathing of trafficking and the repeated media coverage of adopted children with very severe reactive attachment disorder (RAD), fetal alcohol syndrome, and other developmental and psychological issues have created a powerful incentive for the hysterical reorganization of international adoption. It was akin to a lynching. Scapegoats were needed. Suspects were rounded up. The irregularities found in the determination of orphan status just kept surfacing. Adoption was demonized, and ending adoption became a solution for many countries. Was this not throwing the baby out with the bathwater?

The Hague Convention implemented in 2008 after decades of planning was ultimately a rather hysterical attempt to reorganize international adoption and make it more transparent and to prevent trafficking. The treaty has unfortunately created paralyzing bureaucracy and an adoption process that is inefficient, cumbersome, and unnecessarily expensive. Adoption agencies were examined, evaluated, and accredited, and hundreds of agencies that didn't meet the established standard went out of business. While this may have been good in some cases, adoption agencies were not the cause of trafficking. Still, millions of dollars were invested in this process. Trafficking is the result of desperation and social disorganization in countries where there is likely overwhelming poverty, lack of governmental infrastructure, and very little psychosocial support for women so that they can get an education and develop sustaining ways of supporting their families.

A young woman in Ethiopia gets pregnant by rape while earning a small amount of birr (Ethiopian money) carrying water on her head in a town outside of Oromo. Her friends and family are traditional and she is ostracized, stigmatized, and even thrown out on the street because the baby is not legitimate. There is no food to feed the birth mother so she can produce adequate breast milk for the baby. There is no community center to sit down with a social worker to discuss available resources. Depression and lack of opportunity lead to abandonment or relinquishment. The inevitable choice young women are forced to make—to not parent their children—is unacceptable. Some parents walk long distances to bring their babies to an orphanage where they hope they will not be known or recognized and insist that they are not the birth parent of the child but merely a neighbor or acquaintance. Other parents secretly leave their babies in a safe location like a marketplace, police station, or church so that the baby will be found quickly and placed in an orphanage. Local government departments without funding and resources cannot effectively investigate these types of circumstances and there is no developed social welfare and case management system able to intervene and prevent the destruction of the family.

Why we have millions of orphans living in horrific institutions in extremely poor communities in developing countries is a complex social and political quagmire. Much of the attention and expense incurred by U.S. Citizenship and Immigration Services and the U.S. Department of State to establish orphan status is moral and effectively implemented. Yet the Hague Convention on Intercountry Adoption is a labyrinthine, expensive, and bureaucratic accreditation system that may ensure responsible accreditation of adoption agencies but has no effect on child protection or in decreasing the numbers of orphans or ensuring that orphans would have a better life.

For those of us in the adoption profession, this has been a very unsettling time. While we may mourn the steady decline in international adoption, at the same time we ponder the morality of focusing solely on international adoption. A dear friend of mine from high school who was an adoption professional was having troubling moral moments that she shared with me; she felt that her participation in adoption was not right in some way. She spoke of her struggle over many years and said that she couldn't justify her work anymore. She decided to participate in the design and implementation of community-based programs in Ethiopia in an effort to move her moral compass away from the idea of placing orphans in families in faraway countries and toward community building. She felt that family capacity and community strengthening abroad was the highest priority. I had similar feelings. Indeed, many relief organizations believe that adoption should be the last resort for an orphan. Reunification and reintegration of families is their goal. The polarization around this issue was not comfortable. Most of us wanted to be working together for better and creative solutions for orphans. Yet, logically speaking, millions of adoptions whether in-country or intercountry are not possible, and focusing only on adoption as the solution is not a smart and strategic long-range plan to help orphans, though facilitation of international adoption should always remain a high priority.

Globally, UNICEF estimates that 153 million children under the age of eighteen have lost one or both parents and are considered orphans; 18 million children have lost both parents. Adoption is one option to help ensure permanency, but it cannot solve the tragic destiny of millions of children living without parental care in dire circumstances. There is an urgency for us to take care of children around the globe who are barred from living the dignified life they deserve.

What happens to the children left behind? Some are institutionalized and others are forced to live on the street or in refugee camps or as slaves to other families—for example, *restaveks*, a Kreyol term for the thousands of Haitian children who are sent away by their parents to work as domestic servants in the homes of "host families." Around the world children are bought and sold as prostitutes or forced into a life of crime, drug dealing, and alcoholism, and many are child laborers making up a large part of the major workforce of countries abroad. Still others become child soldiers fighting ethnic wars in tyrant-led countries. When families survive, the head of the household may be a child of eight years or even younger. Girls are forced into very early marriages even before they menstruate, robbing them of educational opportunities and choices about their future.

The U.N. Convention on the Rights of the Child, created in 1989, states that every child has a right to safety, health, and an education, as well as the right to participate fully in family, cultural, and social life. The United States and the international community must find permanent solutions to address the international orphan crisis. Effective and innovative strategies need to be implemented and more resources must be devoted to preventing child abandonment and helping families to remain intact or be reunified.

Investment in child welfare systems with trained social workers capable of case management in impoverished countries must be a high priority to strengthen and support families and communities. Families need economic opportunities to make a viable living and social services to help guide them out of poverty. Additionally, access to medical care and psychosocial services and universal free education must be available for all children and their families. Without such support services, families are more likely to be torn apart by poverty and become victims of depression and hopelessness that continue the cycle of child relinquishment and abandonment and contribute to the transmission of intergenerational poverty.

Children currently living in orphanages need professionally trained staff/caretakers who are committed and invested in the psychological welfare of each child. Orphans must be reintegrated into their communities by attending local schools so that they are not isolated and stigmatized. Orphanages should be downsized and be more like group homes, run family-style, and foster care (using the South Korean model) should be introduced as a better alternative to residential care facilities. Governments need to invest in strategic plans to deinstitutionalize the care of orphans, making these programs a shared responsibility of society. Attitudes need to be changed about disabled children from ethnic minorities so that there is inclusion of all children into the fabric of life in all developing countries.

As founder and CEO of Worldwide Orphans Foundation, I have witnessed orphans living in squalid and tragic conditions. Once they age out of the orphanage, they are uneducated and unprepared for life outside the institution; they are destined for poor physical and mental health and dependency on welfare systems rather than becoming independent and capable of creating their own families and developing and contributing their own talents to society.

Realizing that millions of orphans would never be adopted was the reason WWO was founded. The mission of Worldwide Orphans Foundation is to transform the lives of orphaned children and help them to become healthy, independent, productive members of their communities. We accomplish this through a sophisticated, organic, and holistic road map that uses play, creativity, discovery, innovation, community building, local partnerships, needs assessments, and capacity building to achieve outcomes that are closely monitored and tested during the process. The programs are the interventions of this strategic plan and comprise the ever evolving vision of WWO, providing orphans with access to medical care, education, and behavioral safety nets and enrichment.

The programs include an academy for 432 children, kindergarten through grade 5, 25 percent of whom have HIV infection; a comprehensive family HIV/AIDS health center for over two thousand patients (children and families); early intervention, special education, and attachment therapy; camps in Ethiopia, Haiti, and

Vietnam; toy libraries in Bulgaria and Haiti; college assistance for youth in Serbia; sports and recreation in Ethiopia and Haiti; global arts, including dance, music, theater, and writing, in four countries; and a core volunteer/internship program with emissaries called Orphan Rangers. All of the programs are managed and led by in-country professionals who are trained, and their capacity is developed to achieve independence and the ability to train more in-country professionals for enduring change.

I am an adoptive parent of two sweet sons from Ethiopia and Vietnam, but adoption will never be the solution to the global orphan crisis. We must be passionate about our efforts to care for the "children left behind." All children deserve an opportunity to realize their full potential in their country and, indeed, the world. Orphans are strong and powerful and they are capable and proud. They are hardy and deserve a dignified life with respect, love, and a full commitment to their future.

Acknowledgments

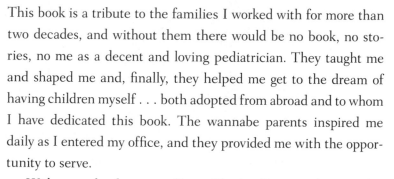

This book is a tribute to the families I worked with for more than two decades, and without them there would be no book, no stories, no me as a decent and loving pediatrician. They taught me and shaped me and, finally, they helped me get to the dream of having children myself . . . both adopted from abroad and to whom I have dedicated this book. The wannabe parents inspired me daily as I entered my office, and they provided me with the opportunity to serve.

With many thanks to my editor at Tarcher/Penguin, Sara Carder, for teaching me how to cooperate. With an even hand she tamed my tendency to not trust and want to fly solo. By the time the book was finished, I was in the flow. Writing is easy compared to the actual and final steps of putting the book together and giving it the professional look and feel it needs. Sara and her assistant, Joanna Ng, and Brianna Yamashita, director of publicity and marketing at Tarcher, knew how to help me cross the finish line.

Grant Ginder, who was my guide at Kuhn Projects, my literary agency, really worked magic for me when I was tearful and doubtful about the writing. I am especially grateful for his friendship and warmth at my darkest moments. I also want to thank Nicole Tourtelot, who took over when Grant left Kuhn Projects. And to David Kuhn goes the highest praise, for thinking of the idea to write the book. At Gramercy Restaurant, over our first and only lunch together, he knew that a collection of essays written by adoptive parents would work best for me. I am so lucky to have met Abigail Pogrebin, who wrote a profile about my work and then thought that David Kuhn would be the literary agent to help me write a book.

Without the inspiration and constant reminders from Melissa Fay Greene that I had a unique voice, I would never have had the confidence to write this book. Her gorgeous writing puts mine to shame, but she tells me that my feelings and observations are worthwhile, and that gives me the courage to write. She is also why I have a lovely son from Ethiopia.

Finally, without the work that I do as founder and CEO of Worldwide Orphans, there would be no focus for the final destiny of this book. The book is about orphans who ended up with permanent families, but the real solution to the orphan crisis is the work of Worldwide Orphans Foundation. WWO is where my heart is forever and ever. The board of directors, the staff, and the stakeholders and donors who support the work we do abroad have loved me through my ups and downs and have trusted and had faith in me to do all that I aspire to do. I am ambitious and have an insatiable appetite for more . . . and WWO is about the realization of more and more and more dreams that ensure that children at risk will have what they need and deserve always.

Friends and family are so dear to me, and they loved me and nurtured me to the final deadline in the fall of 2012. Thanks to

Andrew Vaughan, who was always available to me as he traveled in his car to the boroughs of New York City to serve developmentally delayed children at risk in housing projects. A special thanks to Carol Barash, who I walk with in the Reservation in South Orange, both of us, talking endlessly about our writing in hopes that we will write more and finish all that we start.

Special thanks go to friends who were nice enough to allow me to go off on a riff about the writing and my work anytime that I cared to . . . and I do this a lot: Deborra-lee Furness, Hugh Jackman, Connie Britton, Carla Gugino, Luisella Meloni, David Belle, Andrew Garfield, Emma Stone, Noah Gonzalez, Liz Himelstein, Maggie Greenwald, Nina Lerner, Vince Wiener, David Ivill, Michael Leeds, and my nephew, Gabe Aronson.

There are some endlessly generous colleagues who have become friends who need to be acknowledged: Melissa Baer and Ken Sunshine at Sunshine Sachs and Judith R. King at Morris-King.

What would I do without Toni Monnin's laughter and *bisous*. Love and kisses to Barry Collodi, my executive coach, who saved my life this year.

For scholarly enrichment, I have always gone to Dr. Susan Bissell, the chief of child protection at UNICEF. She likes my blogs, which are sometimes over the top with sentimentality, even when she is terribly jet-lagged in far-off countries delivering keynote addresses.

Thanks to all the social workers at adoption agencies who believed in me and sent me the nicest families to work with all these years. It was the social workers who taught me the nuts and bolts of adoption medicine. Flicka Van Praagh, who likely was in adoption services for forty years, gave me the courage to make adoption medicine my specialty.

I thank the many support personnel who worked in my pediatric offices at Winthrop-University Hospital on Long Island, on East 62nd Street and East 30th Street, who are unsung and who suffered my eternal lack of patience and my perfectionism. Many didn't survive my demands and relentlessly high expectations, but I am so grateful for every bit of their work.

Special thanks to Dr. Sophie Mengistu, Country Director of WWO Ethiopia, who was endlessly generous to the families I worked with as they were adopting from Ethiopia and needed medical intervention for unexpected and sometimes life-threatening medical crises in Addis Ababa.

Finally, I thank Amy Poehler, fellow alumna of the class of 2009 for *Glamour*'s Woman of the Year, who has become a dear and precious girlfriend, with no conditions, a lot of laughter, and fantastic advice, from poetry to Pema to the Gabe Dixon Band to photos of her boys and for sharing the usual human dramas that plague us all. Without her texts, I would be more lonely and as unwanted as a stink bug! I am not sure if I can ever travel to Haiti again without her.

Thanks, Pops, because you always wanted me to write a book and I scoffed at your idea. My brother, Barry, who is long gone now—twenty-seven years—would have been very proud.

"Not only an evocative memoir on East–West adoption but also a bridge to East–West understanding of human rights in China." —AMY TAN

Adopted Girls, Their Journey to America,

and the Search for a Missing Past

REVISED
and
UPDATED

THE LOST

DAUGHTERS

OF CHINA

KARIN EVANS
Foreword by Anchee Min

978-1-58542-676-8 $14.95

another place at the table

kathy harrison

"Touching . . . With the nation's foster care system under scrutiny because of abuse and neglect, the book serves as a reminder of how two selfless souls can literally save kids' lives."
—*People*

978-1-58542-282-1 $14.95

6|13